D0046223

Inside the Carnival

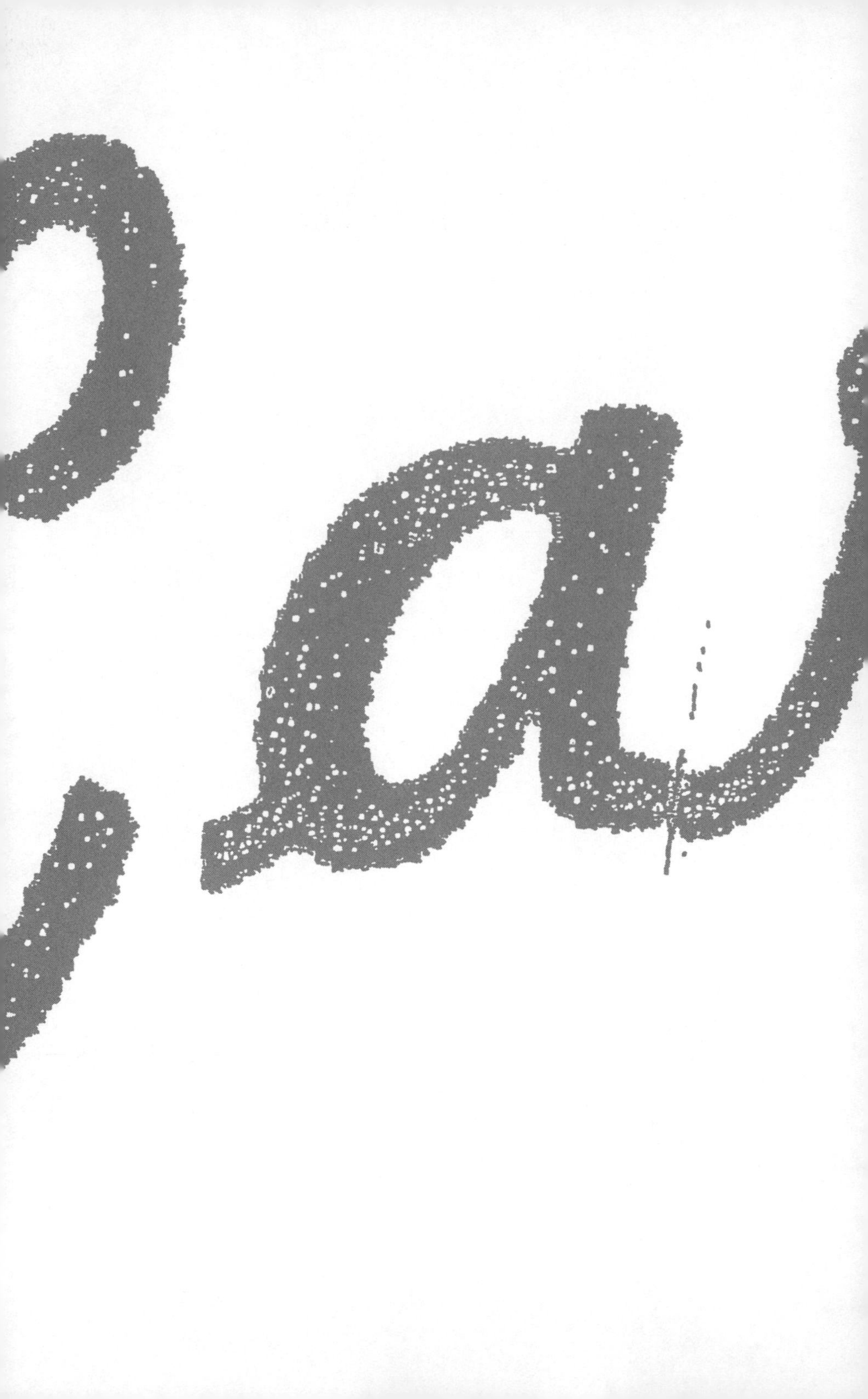

Inside the Carnival

UNMASKING LOUISIANA POLITICS

Wayne Parent

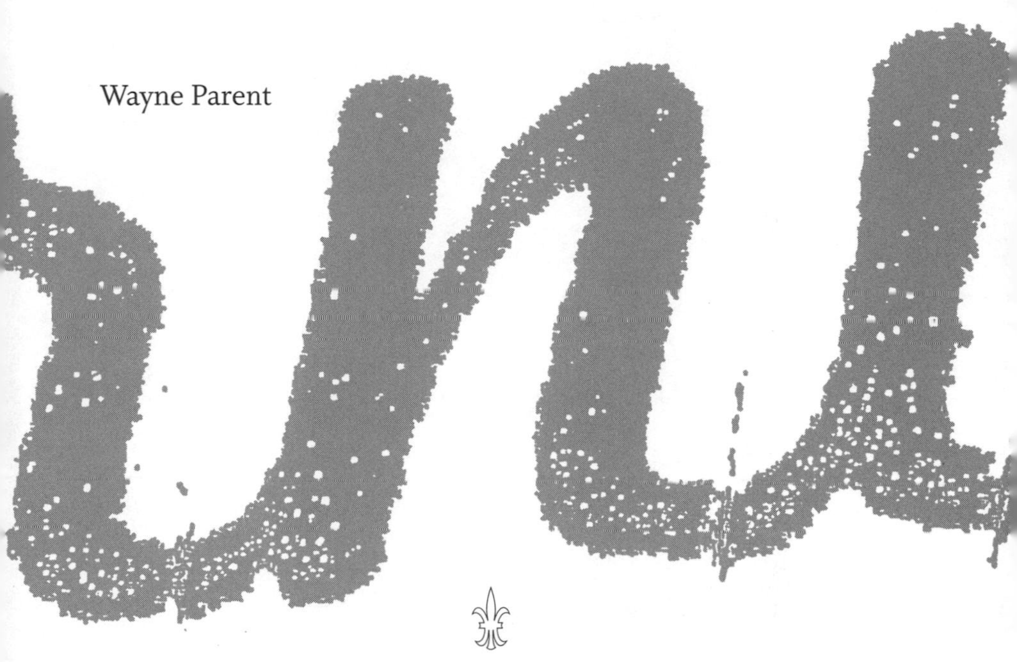

Louisiana State University Press
BATON ROUGE

Manufactured in the United States of America
SECOND PRINTING, 2004

DESIGNER: Andrew Shurtz
TYPEFACE: Whitman
PRINTER AND BINDER: Thomson-Shore, Inc.

Library of Congress Cataloging-in-Publication Data

Parent, Wayne, 1955–
Inside the carnival : unmasking Louisiana politics / Wayne Parent.
p. cm.
Includes bibliographical references and index.
ISBN 0-8071-2938-0 (hardcover : alk. paper)
1. Louisiana—Politics and government—20th century. I. Title.
JK4716.P37 2004
320.4763—dc22 2003027015

The paper in this book meets the guidelines for permanence and durability of the Committee on Production Guidelines for Book Longevity of the Council on Library Resources. ∞

For my Father,

FERRIS JOSEPH PARENT

The reason I love this place

and

For my Mother,

LOUISE THOMAS PARENT
1923–1994

She would have loved this.

Contents

Photographs

Maps and Tables

Preface

I WAS STANDING ON THE BALCONY of a motel in Fort Collins, Colorado, looking east and seeing Nebraska or maybe Kansas, when I realized why I am so drawn to Louisiana. I was about to be offered an assistant professorship of political science at Colorado State and was thinking about what it would be like to live the next phase of my life in the West. As I gazed out over miles and miles of openness, I understood for the first time the notion of Big Sky country. I felt insignificant. The sky, the mountains, the clouds were all overwhelming. I was a dot. I pictured myself driving down Highland Road south of LSU in Baton Rouge, feeling very much a part of the thickness—the trees hanging down, the people, the roaches—all literally connected by the thickness of the air. I wanted to go home.

A few weeks later, I was offered the same job at LSU, and over the next twenty-five years I gradually came to understand intellectually what I always knew emotionally. I had been trained as a social scientist and learned to cringe when I heard comments like "Louisiana politics is a gumbo" and "It's that way because we're just Louisiana." I still cringe. I couldn't just anecdote my way to conclusions. I had to confirm my suspicions honestly and rigorously. I found that the more I looked, the more connections and consistency I saw. Louisiana was always an asterisk in state politics studies, and after a while the asterisks started to line up.

It's just Louisiana? It's a gumbo? Not really answers. Too simple. California is just California. And even Indiana and Iowa exhibit distinct political cultures . . . maybe. Louisiana differences run much deeper and deserve a genuine systematic explanation. Louisiana may be a gumbo, but it's one that needs to be explained.

While it is easy to focus on crazy elections and bizarre shenanigans of flamboyant politicians to describe the character of any state's politics as colorful (although, admittedly, Governors Huey and Earl Long and Edwin Edwards were masters of the game), it is not the individual stories that bear inspection and study. The inspiration for this study is the knowledge that there are a series of distinctions found in Louisiana politics and government that are much wider and much deeper and that, most importantly, can be explained systematically.

If some of our students are to be believed, political scientists seem to make a career of turning something as fascinating as politics into something incredibly boring by making every compelling argument into a series of a thousand iterations of formulas and equations and models and variables. Louisiana politics does not deserve that fate. Hopefully this discussion will contain the solid, satisfying explanations of rigorous social science and the liveliness of all of the juicy stories used to illustrate the points along the way.

Acknowledgments

LOTS OF FOLKS MADE THIS BOOK much better. Michael Henderson, my ridiculously bright graduate assistant and very good friend, worked tirelessly editing and suggesting revisions. Without Mike's help, I'm not sure I would have started or finished it. Brian Thompson's research on Leander Perez and on New Orleans were invaluable to the local politics chapter. In addition, several others helped in a variety of other ways. They are: Gerry Anders, Phillip Ardoin, Cecil Eubanks, Maureen Hewitt, Omar Khalid, Parker Marschall, Richard Moreland, Peter Petrakis, Ellis Sandoz, John Tadayeski, Shaun Mena, Krystal Williams, and Roy Bergeron Jr.

I'd also like to thank my family for their incredible support in this and everything else. They are Ferris, Grace, Dale, Bonnie, and Randy.

Much of what I know about Louisiana politics I learned from people who played a big part in its unfolding. Since 1983 several people have generously given their time to speak to my sophomore-level Louisiana Government class at LSU. I cannot single out any specific lecture, since all of them have melded into my general understanding of Louisiana culture and politics. I want to give heartfelt thanks to these men and women not only for their gift of time and insight to the students in their particular semester, but because those insights have lived on semester after semester as they have been incorporated into subsequent lectures and into this book. Without these individuals' commitment to education, this book could never have been written.

They are United States Senators John Breaux and Mary Landrieu; Governors Edwin Edwards, Charles "Buddy" Roemer, and Mike Foster; Lt. Governors Bobby Freeman, Melinda Schwegmann, and Kathleen Blanco; Attorneys General William Guste and Richard Ieyoub; Secretaries of State Paul Hardy and "Fox" McKeithen; Commissioner of Insurance and Secretary of State Jim Brown; state senators Jay Dardenne, Tom Greene, Melvin "Kip" Holden, John Guidry, and Louis Lambert; state representatives Karen Carter, Melissa Flournoy, E. L. "Bubba" Henry, Michael Jackson, Charles Riddle, and Sharon Weston Broome; state supreme court justice Harry Lemmon; governor's chief of staff Stephen Perry; and governor's staff member Kristy McKearn. In addition, United States district judge Tommy Porteous; political consultants and journalists James Carville, John Maginnis, Marsanne Golsby, James Nickel, Jack Wardlaw, Robert Mann, and Dane Strother and Raymond Strother; and congressional candidate Marjorie McKeithen.

Inside the Carnival

1. Political Culture

The Long Reputation

In the fall of 1991 a sticker reading "Vote for the Crook, It's Important" appeared on car bumpers across the state of Louisiana. The slogan referred to an eye-catching governor's race between colorful, gregarious Cajun governor Edwin Edwards, who had spent most of his third term successfully defending himself in federal court against charges of racketeering, and David Duke, a former state representative universally known for his early career as a grand wizard of the Ku Klux Klan. The specter of these two runoff candidates contending for the highest office in the state was both entertaining and unsettling, like a dark comedy played out to the disturbance of the Louisiana public. Voters could cast their favor for either the image of David Duke gowned in Ku Klux Klan robes and speaking before a flaming cross or the mug shot of Edwin Edwards. Ten years later both Duke and Edwards were in jail. Duke pleaded guilty to mail and tax fraud charges and Edwards stood convicted of a variety of political pastimes including conspiracy, money laundering, fraud, and extortion.

The 1991 election for governor was only the latest in a series of bizarre scenes and anecdotes in Louisiana politics. The reputation for spectacular politics casts a long shadow for the people of Louisiana. Most Louisiana citizens have heard the stories of Huey Long wearing loud suits, breaking every rule of decorum in the United States Senate, and insulting President Franklin Roosevelt. They know about Earl Long's romance with the Bourbon Street stripper Blaze Starr (who, at twenty-three, was forty years younger than he), and they have seen the old newsreels of Earl screaming wildly at the legislature before he suffered a breakdown and was shipped off to a mental hospital. They also know the only story that could top this tale—how Earl maneuvered his way out of the mental hospital to return to the helm of state government. While the race between Edwards and Duke may not have surprised anyone in Louisiana, it was evidence that the political reputation of the state was not going away any time soon.

Perhaps because Louisianians are so familiar with this reputation and the shenanigans from which it sprouts, they are usually a little more forgiving than outsiders in their appraisals of state politics. A quick glance at popular T-shirts is telling: "Louisiana: Third World and Proud of It"; "It's Not the Heat. It's the Stupidity"; and so on. Out-of-state observers are not always as charitable.

The national reputation gelled in the early part of the twentieth century as scholars joined a chorus of journalists, novelists, and politicians in isolating Louisiana politics. In his classic 1949 work *Southern Politics*, V. O. Key singled out the state for special distinction when he titled his chapter on Louisiana "The Seamy Side of Democracy," a clear reference to political corruption.[1] Fifty years later, the title to the Louisiana chapter in Alexander Lamis's *Southern Politics in the 1990s* referred to the uniqueness of politics in Louisiana with the Latin phrase *sui generis*, meaning "one of a kind."[2] There is ample evidence to support both characterizations.

The differences between Louisiana and all of the other states are legion. No other state has a French-based legal system. No other state has an election system where two Democrats or two Republicans can face each other in the final vote on general election day. No other state has had as many constitutions. No other state has such a curiously powerful governor with such curiously weak constitutional prerogatives. Add these and other features to a perhaps unparalleled record of political corruption and the end result is a state that can claim itself systematically, objectively, scientifically unique. Even though their attitudes toward the reputation may diverge, it is obvious to both Louisianians and outsiders—and to laymen and academics—that Louisiana politics is different. These genuine, concrete peculiarities raise questions about the exact nature of the state's oddity and the reasons for it. The reasons for the difference in politics between Louisiana and the other forty-nine states, however, may not be as obvious as the differences themselves.

V. O. Key's Louisiana and Beyond

In almost every category of state politics studies, from constitutions to elections, Louisiana is usually marked by an asterisk denoting a peculiarity or exception to the general rule. This trend of exception appears early in the scholarship. In 1949, V. O. Key, the most influential scholar in characterizing Louisiana, was not shy about his amazement at corruption in the state's politics: "Few would contest the proposition that among its professional politicians of the past two decades Louisiana has had more men who have been in jail, or who should have been, than any other American state. Extortion, bribery, peculation, thievery are not rare in the annals of politics, but in the scale, variety and thoroughness of its operations the Long gang established, after the death of the Kingfish, a record unparalleled in our times."[3] Key was right. Louisiana politics is anything but normal. Yet Key was only voicing in academic circles what was becoming conventional wisdom everywhere else—and in focusing on corruption, he only scratched the surface.

The next landmark book on southern politics, written by Jack Bass and Walter DeVries, was published in 1976, after the successes of the civil rights movement and the Republican Party in the south. In *The Transformation of Southern Politics: Social Change and Political Consequence since 1945*, Bass and DeVries define the Louisiana culture more broadly than merely in terms of corruption: "Louisiana politics remain an exotic mixture of the populist philosophy, reawakened and perpetuated by the Longs; racism, whose intensity peaked in the 1960s, the cultural clash between the fun-loving tolerant Cajuns of French-Catholic ancestry in the south and the moralistic, Anglo-Saxon Baptists in the north; a black electorate that is growing stronger and more sophisticated; and the spicy urban culture of New Orleans and its suburbs."[4]

Tyler Bridges, a Pulitzer Prize–winning journalist who worked for the *New Orleans Times-Picayune*, summed up the state's political culture in his 2001 book on Edwin Edwards and gambling in Louisiana:

> Louisiana is our most exotic state. It is religious and roguish, a place populated by Cajuns, Creoles, Christian Conservatives, rednecks, African Americans, and the white working-class New Orleanians known as "Yats." While northern Louisiana is mostly Protestant and conservative, southern Louisiana, settled by French Catholics, is noted for its love of good food, good music, and good times. Laissez les Bons Temps Rouler—Let the Good Times Roll—is the unofficial motto. Louisiana is rich in outrageous stories and colorful characters. It is notably poor in the realm of political ethics.[5]

Like Bass and DeVries, recent political science scholars have tended to emphasize the "exotic" volatility inherent in Louisiana culture more than the corruption, although this exoticism is normally delineated in an anything-but-exotic way.

Although the political reputation of Louisiana is certainly a reputation for corruption, corruption is only one part of a much broader pattern of peculiarity. The constitutions, the governor's office, the legislature, the courts, the voting system, and even the local governments are immersed in a common political culture that has shaped and defined them. Viewed more broadly, the political culture of Louisiana is a culture of volatility, instability, and constant competition.

Beyond the Cliches: Political Culture as Explanation

What is the distinct political culture of Louisiana and where does it come from? Is Louisiana corrupt because Louisianians are just born that way? Is Louisiana highly competitive and participatory because of something in the water? While there may very well be something peculiar in the water, this probably yields little explanatory power for the political oddity situated between Texas and Mississippi. If the political culture in Louisiana is truly unique, there should be concrete reasons for that uniqueness. These reasons or circumstances should logically connect with the particular culture.

Louisiana has peculiar politics because of the state's distinct political culture; Louisiana has a distinct political culture because of a unique arrangement of immigration patterns and geographical characteristics that have influenced the state's historical development. Significant works on political culture, including Alexis de Tocqueville's groundbreaking work on American political culture, associate these factors with the development of a political heritage.[6] Immigration patterns will be the factor I stress the most in this study, because that factor has had the most lasting impact in the state. Louisiana is the home of three distinct groups of immigrants: northern Europeans, Africans, and southern Europeans. Their coexistence, as much as the individual character of each group, has had a most profound effect on the Louisiana culture, and by extension, on Louisiana politics.

While a unique pattern of immigration provides the centerpiece for understanding Louisiana politics, the geography of the state plays a supporting role. Louisiana is situated in a region of enormous natural benefit. First, it is located at the mouth of the Mississippi River, where New Orleans has become the largest inland port in the country. Second, the state possesses great natural resources. The discovery of oil in the beginning of the twentieth century added to and exaggerated some already existing characteristics of the Louisiana political culture.

Taken together, these attributes provide the groundwork for defining the unique culture that produces such a unique brand of politics. All are of course intertwined but for the sake of clarity will be discussed separately.

Sources of Political Culture

De Tocqueville's *Democracy in America* describes the sources of political culture and is one particularly relevant work that manages to be both fascinating and rigorous. Even though it was written in 1848, it remains arguably the best-known and most respected book on American political culture. The explanation that de Tocqueville provides will be taught in hundreds of history and political science courses every semester well into the twenty-first century.

De Tocqueville perceives a single overarching American political culture. He argues that American political culture is unlike any in the rest of the world. According to his explanation, America is a nation of possessive individualists where the concern for the individual and individual material possessions is paramount. De Tocqueville's reasoning has withstood the test of time and is used today to help explain things like the fact that McDonald's, Starbucks, and Nike are in every corner of the earth, or why there is an almost visceral revulsion when the word socialism is voiced in America.

De Tocqueville not only describes the culture, he explains the reasons for it. He ascribes the uniqueness of the American political culture to three concrete historical circumstances. First, the people who settled and dominated the founding of America were opportunists from abroad. Second, Americans form an individualistic culture because of the geography of the place—isolated from the rest of the world. Third, the abundant resources of the land allow for individual prosperity. The people and the geography form the basis for the political culture.

The result? A culture "obsessed with freedom"—rugged individualists who move from place to place and exploit the seemingly endless natural resources.[7] These opportunists were isolated from the rest of the world, so they could set up a government designed to keep the people from getting in each other's way. The general model that de Tocqueville formulates, connecting historical circumstances to political culture, has led to several sound studies of the American political culture. It is difficult to use a full, rich, ambitious masterpiece like de Tocqueville's work as a model for this study of Louisiana; however, de Tocqueville's logic—that the circumstances of a place define a political culture—is too suitable and too useful to ignore.

From People to Politics

Another often-referenced study is Daniel Elazar's *American Federalism: A View from the States*, which examines variations in political cultures *within* the United States.[8] This work is a helpful complement to de Tocqueville's because it examines characteristics that differentiate cultures on a smaller scale. While de Tocqueville sought to explain the uniqueness of the whole of American culture, Elazar sought to explain regional variations within that culture. Why do states differ? His work is grounded in the idea that cultural differences *within the United States* are due to different immigration patterns in the various states.

Like de Tocqueville's discussion of the people who immigrated to America and eventually formed the United States government, Elazar's argument is that political cultures within the states are determined by attitudinal baggage carried with the people who moved into those states. He finds that states can be roughly grouped into three categories, based on the people who settled them. Cecil Eubanks, in a chapter on southern culture in a book on southern politics,[9] presents a clear summary of the three Elazar categories that can be briefly quoted here.

The first set of state cultures was established by English Puritans who "brought their moralistic political culture with them as they moved westward from New England across New York into northern Pennsylvania, Ohio, and most of Michigan, Wisconsin, Minnesota, and Iowa, establishing, along with their Scandinavian counterparts, a greater New England." The second group of American state cultures derived from non-Puritan English immigrants and German settlers who "occupied the middle states in the colonies and migrated into southern Pennsylvania and central Ohio, as well as Indiana, Illinois, and Missouri, reinforced by immigrants from western Europe." These settlers brought with them a highly individualistic culture, much like the one de Tocqueville describes as the dominant American culture. The third group involves states closer to Louisiana: "The southern colonies were settled by an Old World landed gentry, intent on perpetuation of a plantation slave system at the exclusion not only of slaves, but of individual small property holders. These inhabitants of Virginia, the Carolinas, and Georgia moved westward into Alabama and Mississippi, taking their traditional culture with them. *Louisiana, which was settled by the French, shared this same political culture.*"[10]

Eubanks continues with a summary of the predominant southern political culture: "As its name implies, the traditionalistic political culture looks to the past, a pre-industrial past, of strong social and family bonds. Government has an important role in this culture, the maintenance of traditional order; but citizen participation is limited to a paternalistic elite."[11] A starting point, then, is to examine the whole of Louisiana as part of the traditionalistic culture that Elazar says characterizes all of the states in the American South.

Way Down South

To many observers, whether residents or outsiders, Louisiana is first and foremost a southern state. Even though most of its notoriety—and much of the remainder of this discussion—focuses on how Louisiana differs from other states in the South, the distinctiveness of the Louisiana culture in the United States begins with the fact that it is one of only eleven states that bear all of the pride, scars, and other psychological and physical baggage of a southern traditionalistic culture. Louisiana is one of the five southern states—the Deep South states—where these characteristics are magnified and are most persisting. Indeed, much of Louisiana was settled by an old world landed gentry from Europe bringing a traditionalistic culture intent on preserving itself. Although the political culture in Louisiana is much more complex than simply that fact, it is a logical place to begin. Any understanding of Louisiana must start by lining it up especially with its Deep South neighbors Mississippi, Alabama, Georgia, and South Carolina, as well as the other seven states that composed the Confederacy. Louisiana is, after all, way down south.

As a distinct region in the United States, the South exhibits a different kind of politics from that of its northern and western neighbors. Indeed, in important ways, the South has a political culture unheard of throughout the rest of the nation. But the people of the South, and the people of Louisiana, bear another important element to their cultural heritage. The most renowned southern historian of our time, C. Vann Woodward, portrays the South in inimitable words that are hard to ignore. He examines and explains the rebellion, revolution, frustration and resentment that characterize southern politics, all of which can be found in the politics of Louisiana. Woodward sums up this southern predicament in his classic book *The Burden of Southern History:*

> For the inescapable facts of history were that the South had repeatedly met with frustration and failure. It had learned that it was to be faced with economic, social, and political problems that refused to yield to all the ingenuity, patience, and intelligence that a people could bring to bear upon them. It had learned to accommodate itself to conditions that it swore it would never accept, and it had learned the taste left in the mouth by the swallowing of one's own words. It had learned to live for long decades in quite un-American poverty, and it had learned the equally un-American lesson of submission. For the South had undergone an experience that it could share with no other part of America—though it is shared by nearly all the peoples of Europe and Asia—the experience of military defeat, occupation, and reconstruction.[12]

The South's distinctiveness begins well before these historical developments, as Elazar indicates, in the traditionalistic culture brought to the region by those who settled there. The impact of this traditionalistic culture in most of the South has been wide-ranging, especially when it is combined with the effects of the Civil War on the same people in the same region. There are two standard reference works on southern culture that, like Elazar, view the settlement by old world landed gentry, trying to preserve an agrarian culture, as the key to understanding the South. Both, of course, are also cognizant of the impact of the Civil War.

These classic books are W. J. Cash's *The Mind of the South*, published in 1941, and *I'll Take My Stand: The South and the Agrarian Tradition*, published in 1930 by a group of authors who called themselves simply "Twelve Southerners."[13] Both works have been the subject of several scholarly seminars and colloquia. Indeed, both have been revisited as the subjects of published fifty-year retrospectives. They provide nice contrasts and together allow a fairly complete portrayal of the scholarship on southern culture.

The Cash book is the most biting. It makes some southerners furious. To Cash, the key to understanding the South is the relationship between the landed aristocracy (former plantation owners, other large landowners) and poorer white people, tenant farmers and otherwise. He sees the upper classes as cynically creating a bond with lower-income white people by emphasizing their shared culture and fueling the fires of racism by contrasting them with their black counterparts—in effect saying, "You may be poor, but most important, you're white." This strategy keeps poor white tenant farmers from joining with former slave tenant farmers to work together for rights, privileges, and better working conditions. United, poorer whites and blacks would be a potent political and social force. Divided along racial lines, especially with poor whites bonding psychologically with upper-class whites, the social and economic order can be preserved and those who dominate society can remain in place.

To make matters worse, these landed gentry who controlled southern society are filled with guilt about slavery, are clinging to a lost cause and falsely romanticizing their past glories. By design, they serve as role models to the masses of poorer whites. The result, according to Cash, is a "Savage Ideal"—a southern character defined by the guilt-ridden aristocracy and copied by the impoverished, uneducated, manipulated white masses. Cash does not indulge in southern polite distance when he concludes his book with this description of southern culture:

> Proud, brave, honorable by its lights, courteous, personally generous, loyal, swift to act, often too swift, but signally effective, sometimes terrible, in its actions—such was the South at its best. And such at its best it remains today, despite the great falling away in some of its virtues. Violence, intolerance, aversion and suspicion toward new ideas, an incapacity for analysis, an inclination to act from feeling rather than from thought, an exaggerated individualism and a too narrow concept of social responsibility, attachment to fictions and false values, above all too great attachment to racial values and a tendency to justify cruelty and injustice in the name of those values, sentimentality and a lack of realism—these have been its characteristic vices in the past. And, despite changes for the better, they remain its characteristic vices today.[14]

This is certainly not a view of the South that most white southerners would find appealing or accurate. Yet if Cash was criticized for several aspects of his monumental work, his ideas resonated and became one cornerstone of the definition of white southern culture. The hallmarks—violence, intolerance, racism, and holding on to the status quo—remain accepted stereotypes of southern whites.

On the other hand, *I'll Take My Stand* offers a characterization of the South that is much more palatable to most white southerners. The authors were mainly literary scholars at Vanderbilt University reacting to the industrialization and modernization of the South. The most prominent member of the group was Robert Penn Warren who spent some of his career at Louisiana State University and was the author of the novel *All the King's Men*—a book normally interpreted as a thinly veiled reference to the career of Louisiana's Huey Long.

I'll Take My Stand defines southern culture in terms of adamant agrarianism. These writers emphasize that the southern agrarian way of life is superior to industrialized, modern society because it upholds traditional values, especially religious values, and it allows labor to be fulfilling rather than assembly-line monotony. Industrialization drives the need for consumption, which in turn leads to the primacy of commercial interests over all other values. Family relationships and friendships are overwhelmed by the need for money and become dictated and defined by commercial interests rather than more nurturing, caring "family values." In the *Encyclopedia of Southern Culture,* George Tindall encapsulates the Twelve Southerners' version of southern culture in Donald Davidson's words, "family, blood-kinship, clanship, folkways, custom, community."[15]

Yet the state that boasts of Bourbon Street and so readily embraces gambling as a tool for economic development makes an odd fit with the traditionalistic culture of the South. This convoluted relationship between Louisiana culture and southern "Dixie" culture is symbolized in some clever historical ironies that bear mentioning. While many Louisianians are aware that their most famous politician, Huey Long, was the son of an abolitionist, the ultimate irony to most die-hard Confederates in Louisiana concerns the most infamous United States general in the Civil War, William Tecumseh Sherman. Sherman, whose troops burned their way from Atlanta to the Atlantic, became a symbol of the Union army's destruction of the South. In fact, even Georgia's tourist website notes: "If the question was asked, 'Who was and still is the most hated and despised man in the history of Georgia,' the response would be William Tecumseh Sherman. From the onset of hostilities in the Atlanta Campaign on May 6, 1864 and the March to the Sea ending two days before Christmas 1864 with him capturing Savannah, no one created more destruction. As a result of his successful campaign in Georgia, the Confederacy was split in two and deprived of much needed supplies, ending the war quickly with a Union victory."[16] In Louisiana, however, William Tecumseh Sherman is also known as the first president of Louisiana State University. Louisiana's uneasy relationship with the Confederacy is symbolized by that and much more.

Oddly enough, the name "Dixie," the most endearing term for the South, may well have some unseemly Louisiana roots. Despite its use by southern traditionalists who pride themselves on family values, it may well have found its origin in the French name for the amount of money needed to hire a prostitute in the least "southern" of cities in the Deep South, New Orleans. One dictionary explains it this way: "Ten dollar notes issued by the Citizens Bank of Louisiana before the Civil War bore the French 'dix,' ten, on the reverse side and were consequently known as 'dixes' or 'dixies'. Hence Louisiana and eventually the South in general came to be known as the land of 'dixies' or 'dixies land.'"[17] Although this particular explanation of the origin of the word *Dixie* is widespread, it is not at all conclusive and remains controversial.

Behind these anecdotal ironies linger cultural distinctions. Louisiana's political culture includes many of the attributes of most political cultures in the southern part of the United States, but important differences remain. Elazar's lumping together of Louisiana with all of the other southern states, while understandable, is a bit misleading. Louisiana may fall primarily into the traditionalistic culture, inasmuch as it is southern, but Louisiana experienced much more complicated immigration patterns than most southern states. Although Elazar combines the French Bourbon immigrants in south Louisiana with the northern European immigrants in central and north Louisiana in a single political culture, a distinction exists between the two and is worth examining.

The People: Northern European Louisianians

Unquestionably, the southernness of Louisiana runs throughout the state, from Lake Providence in the far northeast corner to Marsh

Island, where Louisiana blurs into the Gulf of Mexico. Even so, north Louisiana most readily and vividly fits the standard of southern culture. In many ways north Louisiana can be viewed as the most southern part of the state, blending well with the rest of the Deep South. In the northern piney hills around Ruston one feels culturally closer to Mississippi than to fellow Louisianians living along Bayou Teche. From politics to food, north Louisiana seems more like a southern state than does the French coast. It is more chicken-fried steak and barbeque than jambalaya and etouffée.

The immigration patterns in north Louisiana produced a political culture much like that found in most of Mississippi, Alabama, Georgia, and South Carolina. Patterns of immigration of people from northern European ancestry, including many Scottish and Irish immigrants, define much of north Louisiana. These patterns occur throughout the American South and provide the basis for its traditionalistic political culture.

Anglo-Americans settled in Louisiana, particularly north Louisiana, in increasing numbers throughout the early 1800s. Outnumbered seven to one by Franco-Americans in 1806, by 1830 Anglo-Americans had cut the gap to two to one. These settlers continued to surge into the state and in the mid-1840s they began to outnumber Franco-Americans. They brought with them the culture of the southern United States, Protestant religion, and a political mentality that distinguished them markedly from their French predecessors. Cultural variation brought political distrust: "Not surprisingly, this migration of Anglo-Americans into Louisiana, and the political challenge that these newcomers offered to the hegemony of the previously dominant ethnic group, resulted in the growth of distrust, hostility, and ethnocultural conflict between French and Anglo-Americans which was often manifest in the political arena."[18]

The People: African Louisianians

The most prominent demographic characteristic of all of the five states of the Deep South is the proportion of citizens with African ancestry. The percentage of African Americans in the United States is 13. According to the 2000 Census, five of the six states with the largest proportions of African Americans are Deep South states—Mississippi with 36 percent, Louisiana with 32 percent, South Carolina with 30 percent, Georgia with 29 percent, and Alabama with 26 percent. (The one non–

Deep South state of the six was Maryland, with 28 percent.) Even though southern blacks vary tremendously in several socioeconomic traits, black culture in Louisiana is probably the most politically self-conscious.

When prominent historian Lisa Baker described New Orleans in her landmark work on school desegregation in the city, she said that "its family tree looked like no other in the United States" and referred to Gwendolyn Midlo Hall's comment that in spirit New Orleans is "the most African city in the United States."[19] They were probably right.

Just as African roots are obvious in New Orleans, they can be seen and felt in rural areas as well. As map 1-A (Appendix 1) shows, the African American population in Louisiana is most concentrated in Orleans Parish and in rural parishes along the Mississippi River Delta. In addition to Orleans, the Louisiana parishes with the largest percentage of African Americans are East Carroll, Madison, and Tensas in northeast Louisiana and St. James and St. Helena in the southeast, all rural places.

Since the term "immigration pattern" is not appropriate for the arrival of most African Americans to Louisiana and the South, a brief history of the slow emergence of blacks as a force in Louisiana and southern politics is necessary. The African American culture in Louisiana is a product of a totally independent set of circumstances than the European immigration patterns.

Outside New Orleans and a community of Franco-Africans associated with Melrose Plantation near Natchitoches, black history in Louisiana is mostly the same as black history in the remainder of the South. In New Orleans, however, a black Creole population had a major impact on the culture of the city. The term Creole itself is controversial. Sometimes it is used to denote only French and Spanish mixtures.[20] More often, however, it refers to people in New Orleans who "traced their origins to eighteenth-century unions of French and Spanish settlers with indigenous Indian women, African slaves, and black refugees from later political upheavals in the Caribbean."[21] Unlike most American blacks, Creoles were normally Catholic, spoke mostly French, and enjoyed much more financial success than most of slave society precisely because many Creoles were not themselves slaves.[22] Despite the restrictions on black society by the Louisiana government, black Creoles in New Orleans thrived. Most of the rest of the black population in Louisiana, however, experienced the same hardships and indignities that blacks faced in the remainder of the South.

Charles Grenier summarizes the experiences of blacks in Louisiana and the South since the Civil War as follows:

> Louisiana's history is typical of the Deep South states for the period under investigation. American blacks were given the vote when slavery was abolished after the Civil War during the reconstruction program of 1867. Federally designated military rulers supervised the registration of over 700,000 blacks, slightly more than the number of whites registered at that time. . . . Three years later the U.S. Congress passed the 14th and 15th amendments to the constitution, specifying that the right to vote, "shall not be denied . . . on account of race, color or previous condition of servitude." These amendments provided a constitutional basis for a central political authority in the matter of universal suffrage, but it left the states almost totally free to regulate political parties, elections and suffrage.
>
> Consequently, the various southern states began passing laws aimed specifically at the disqualification of the black electorate, with such requirements as literacy tests, good-character tests, poll taxes, property qualifications, and civil understanding tests. The counterrevolution against the abolitionists also included the formation of a single party political system, the Southern Democratic Party, which became the absolute ruling party in the region. This led to the development of the most formidable barrier of all, the so-called white primary. Southern Democrats moved to disallow blacks as members, rationalized by a series of statutory revisions at the state level. Since nomination by the Democratic party was tantamount to election, debarment from the nominating process was the equivalent of disenfranchisement. Statewide rules at the county and city committee level restricted the black to nonpartisan and special elections where his Republican vote was a mere gesture. Louisiana remained a one-party system up until 1980, with the election of the first Republican governor in 100 years.
>
> Superimposed on this quasi-legal political structure were the forces of physical coercion, fear, political apathy, economic coercion, discrimination, and the lack of political organization, among other things, all acting to curtail black political participation. By 1900 the black vote in the South had virtually disappeared. In 1930 the black population in Louisiana was around 50 percent and only one percent were regis-

tered to vote. In 1980, 30 percent of the population was black and 70 percent of them were registered. The re-enfranchisement process began in the late 1940s with the Supreme Court invalidation of the white primary, and culminated with the Voting Rights Act of 1965. The Voting Rights Act departed from the pattern set by the 1957, 1960, and 1964 Civil Rights Acts which depended almost entirely upon private litigation, by providing for direct federal action to enable blacks to register and vote. The Act suspended literacy tests and other discriminatory voter registration tests. Federal Examiners were assigned to the various states to supervise registration in problem counties. And federal observers were assigned to monitor elections in counties where examiners served under the Act.[23]

The African American political culture in Louisiana is a durable culture of abiding black consciousness and unity as a result of two centuries of continuous, institutional, deep-rooted, and calculated discrimination. Understandably, this culture is not defined by social conservatism or social liberalism. Instead the African American political culture, currently, is unified by a lack of trust of the majority political establishment and a desire and need to advance the group as a whole.

While blacks are dominant players in several cities and key players in several states, the impact of African Americans in Louisiana's political culture may well be more powerful than in any other state. Blacks are more urban in Louisiana than in other southern states where their numbers and proportions are the highest. They are therefore more active and empowered than in other Deep South states. A longstanding established black middle class in New Orleans serves to accentuate the already raised political activism. Indeed, in 1860 the black population in New Orleans was split closely between 13,000 slaves and 11,000 free blacks.[24] Although the free black population was increasingly constrained as the Civil War neared, a considerable black middle class had begun to develop very early in Louisiana's history.

The impact of an empowered African American electorate, after decades of frustration, can have a snowball effect. When black candidate "Dutch" Morial was elected mayor in majority white New Orleans in 1977, black voter registration skyrocketed.[25] By the end of the twentieth century African American voter registration and participation in Louisiana was almost the same as white participation and registration.[26] Although no African American has yet been elected to statewide office, African Americans are a relatively cohesive, significant force in Louisiana politics and are one of the three major broad ethnic groups whose interaction forms the basis of Louisiana's political culture.

The People: Southern European Louisianians

When the Creole French candidate for the U.S. Senate, Charles Gayarré, won in 1835, one commentator made the following note: "We have raised up in our Louisiana politics an element unknown in other states—an element difficult to manage or estimate its effect—I mean Creolism—a kind of national native feeling—principally operating on moderate natives of French origin."[27] Indeed, perhaps more than any other characteristic, the French-based culture of south Louisiana skews Louisiana's fit with the American South.

In his landmark article "The Secession Election in Louisiana," historian Charles Dew begins with a striking declaration: "Of all of the states in the Lower South, Louisiana seemed the most firmly attached to the Union."[28] He points first to New Orleans:

> New Orleans, the South's largest and most cosmopolitan city, had strong ties with the upper Mississippi Valley, and her shipping and financial activities were closely associated with the major eastern ports, New York in particular. In addition, the city's business elite had a large and prominent northern-born element, and many of these influential businessmen were, at best, lukewarm to the secessionist cause. New Orleans' sizable immigrant population also displayed a notable lack of enthusiasm for secession during the 1850s. In the opinion of Senator John Slidell, the master manipulator of the state Democratic organization, the Irish and the Germans in the Crescent City were "at heart abolitionists."[29]

Dew then speaks of south Louisiana more generally as he contrasts it with the northern part of the state. "Secessionist sentiment ran strongest in the cotton parishes along the Mississippi and Red Rivers, districts characterized by large plantations and a heavy concentration of slaves. In the Delta parishes of southern Louisiana, however, the protective federal tariff on sugar tempered enthusiasm for secession."[30]

As Dew points out, the immigration patterns in New Orleans are not as obviously part of the traditionalistic southern culture as the remainder of the South. Although Dew concentrates on the differences between the agricultural economies in north and south Louisiana, immigration patterns were important as well and helped defined south Louisiana as much less of a traditional southern culture.

Many outward signs point to this less traditional, less southern culture. The celebrity of New Orleans and south Louisiana rests mainly on spicy food and music, but the cultural differences between north and south run much deeper.

Two maps of Louisiana speak volumes (see Appendix 1). Map 1-B shows parish-by-parish religious affiliation. All but four parishes are majority Catholic or majority Baptist (not just Protestant, but Baptist). The top half of the state, the "Dixie" half, is Baptist, while a triangle of parishes in the lower half is Catholic. Map 1-C shows French ancestry by parish. Again, the southern part of the state is clearly distinct.

The French ancestry of Louisiana has a variety of sources. French colonists settled in the delta along the southern portion of the Mississippi River and particularly in New Orleans. The French colony included an Old World–style traditional elite. Other European immigrants, including Spanish colonists and settlers of the so-called German Coast along the Mississippi River above New Orleans, were assimilated into the dominant French culture of the time and took on the language. However, much of the French ancestry found in south Louisiana is a result of migration of thousands of French settlers from an area called Acadia, in what is now Nova Scotia. The history of this migration is romanticized in the popular Henry Wadsworth Longfellow poem *Evangeline*, which in turn is memorialized by Longfellow-Evangeline State Historic Site near St. Martinville. The journey of the Acadians to Louisiana was not an easy one.

In the early 1600s, colonists from France were among the first Europeans to settle in what is now North America. When England obtained possession of Nova Scotia in 1713, there were many attempts to make these people English subjects. After years of often violent resistance, thousands of French Acadians were deported in 1755. Many eventually migrated to Louisiana. By the early 1800s, thousands had made their way to the southern parishes of the state.

These immigrants brought with them a history and a view of government unlike those of the old landed gentry in the northern part of the state, and unlike the African American history of slavery. True, the Acadian political culture was not imbued with the almost complete lack of trust inherent in an African slave culture. However, given its history of political expulsion, it was also not as traditionalistic and protective of the status quo as the northern European political culture formed by the immigrants to north Louisiana.

The political attitudinal effects of the difference in immigration patterns between north and south Louisiana Europeans is described well by David Landry and Joseph Parker: "A generally more tolerant attitude prevails throughout South Louisiana. The sale of alcoholic beverages on Sundays has never been an issue there, and gambling has never been an issue there, although it [was] illegal by state statute." Indeed, *before gambling was legalized* in the state, "According to Marc R. Gore, senior intelligence analyst with the Louisiana State Police, Criminal Intelligence Section, illegal gambling [was] the state's third largest industry, with a value of $244,695,000."[31]

The greater propensity to support gambling in the southern part of the state appeared clearly in the 1997 parish-by-parish vote on video poker. Of the thirty-one majority Catholic parishes—those that roughly define southern European south Louisiana—twenty-one voted for video poker, while of the twenty-nine majority Baptist parishes in northern European north Louisiana, only eight did so.

Greater support for various forms of gambling and more liberal views on the sale of alcohol are part of a broad pattern. As Landry and Parker note, "the contrast between North and South Louisiana was recently demonstrated by the referendum on the 1974 Constitution. The constitution lacked a prohibition against state support for parochial schools, and it contained a strongly worded provision on equal rights."[32] North Louisiana voted heavily against the constitution.

Most Louisianians would quickly recognize and acknowledge the difference in the two cultures on social issues—the more conservative "Bible Belt" north and the more liberal "Cajun" south—but the most conspicuous political difference between the northern and southern cultures may be more surprising. It is in race relations. "Largely because of the Latin tradition of tolerance, racism was rarely as intense or, one might argue, never as institutionalized in South Louisiana as it was in other parts of the South.

In the French parishes, for example, a higher percentage of blacks were registered to vote prior to the 1965 Voting Rights Act than in any other area in the South. Nor did the Ku Klux Klan find much support in South Louisiana primarily because the Klan is anti-Catholic as well as antiblack."[33]

Other, more recent writers have concluded the same thing. Stephan Caldas in his study of voting patterns in Louisiana in the 1990s concludes that south Louisiana Catholic voters were less likely than their counterparts in north Louisiana to support the racially charged rhetoric found in the David Duke campaigns. Caldas argues that in south Louisiana, Catholicism in combination with a "Latin tradition of tolerance" formed the basis for greater racial tolerance.[34]

More strong evidence of different racial attitudes between north and south Louisiana appears in a map found in Earl and Merle Black's *Politics and Society in the South*. It displays county-by-county voting percentages by blacks in the South before the 1965 Voting Rights Act.[35] Acadian south Louisiana appears as distinctly more racially tolerant than either north Louisiana or the Deep South in general.

The case for relatively relaxed racial attitudes in south Louisiana is supported not only by statistical data but in many anecdotal ways as well. The blending of these southern European Americans and African Americans politically and culturally in South Louisiana is obvious. Any observer of shades of skin color at any place where races come together—from a zydeco festival to the oil fields to the legislature—is struck by the variety of and lack of clear visible distinction between the races.

In sum, most Louisianians readily see and acknowledge the differences in social attitudes between the northern and southern parts of the state. The social and cultural liberalism of south Louisiana is most visibly reflected in alcohol and gambling issues but clearly extends to racial issues as well. It is not just the food or the music. It is an entirely different cultural heritage.

The People Form a Disorderly Democracy

Louisiana politics is a constant game of heavy competition, and the first feature of the Louisiana political culture is a disorderly, unstable democracy among three distinct, unmistakable ethnic groups shaped through early immigration patterns. The three main ethnic groups are not significant because they define three voting blocs. They often do not. North and south Louisiana Europeans will often vote together against African Americans, as in the 1995 and 1999 elections for governor in which black candidates Cleo Fields and William Jefferson received little white support, north or south, against Mike Foster. In a *New Orleans Times-Picayune* exit poll of the 1995 race, 96 percent of black respondents said that they voted for Fields, while 84 percent of white respondents were for Foster.[36]

On the other hand, southern European and African voters will often vote mainly together, as in the political victory of Edwin Edwards over David Duke in 1991 (see map 1-D, Appendix 1). Almost as often, the groups do not neatly define three voting blocs at all, as in the cases of most of the recent elections for the U.S. Senate, including the 1996 race between Democrat Mary Landrieu and Republican "Woody" Jenkins (see map 1-E). The map of Duke-Edwards shows some concentration of the support for Duke in north Louisiana, but it also includes a few south Louisiana parishes such as Livingston, Washington, and St. Bernard. The map of the Landrieu-Jenkins election, on the other hand, shows much more dispersion of support across the state. (Of course, the fact that Jenkins won a broader spectrum of parishes than Duke seems at least partly attributable to the fact that Jenkins-Landrieu was a near dead heat, whereas Duke-Edwards was a runaway for Edwards.)

The three groups, therefore, should not be considered voting blocs, because they have a much broader effect. These are ethnic groups with strong group consciousness and a lack of trust in other groups for extended periods of time—thus, the volatility. The existence of these three well-defined, highly self-conscious groups in Louisiana always keeps Louisiana politics unsteady and on guard. These groups keep the political footing in Louisiana as soft as its swampy terrain. More than any other characteristic of the state, they create a culture that is volatile, unsettled, and always highly competitive.

Louisiana's three major ethnic groups set this pattern for an unstable democracy early on. Well before the impact of oil and gas resources on the political culture of the state, Louisiana elites were manipulating and coercing political groups openly and obviously.

The infamous 1896 gubernatorial election is a spectacular example of a political culture in which no one group dominates, the pursuit of power is ruthless, and the victors consolidate their position—until the next competitive, tumultuous election. It is a particularly instructive example because it illustrates the fluidity of the coalitions of ethnic groups and underlines the fact that it is the lack of a single enduring dominant political group that defines the volatile nature of Louisiana's democracy.

In 1896, African Americans aligned with some central and north Louisiana whites—a coalition that would occur only infrequently during the whole course of the following century. The two main candidates for governor were both from St. Mary Parish. They were John Newton Pharr and Murphy J. Foster (whose grandson would be elected governor a century later, in 1995 and 1999). Pharr's "Fusion" ticket had the support of blacks statewide and of white farmers in north Louisiana. Foster's Bourbon Democrat ticket, which had been fairly entrenched in power since Reconstruction, was losing popular support rapidly. This tenuous hold on power caused a fierce campaign against the Fusion ticket, including everything from name-calling ("John Nigger Pharr") to lynching to outrageous vote fraud. The Bourbons won. The official returns from the pro-Bourbon parishes are astounding. In Bossier, Foster received 3,464 official votes to Pharr's 58; in West Feliciana, Foster's vote total was 3,093 to Pharr's 1 vote; in East Carroll and Tensas, Foster was recorded with 2,635 and 1,968 votes while Pharr, incredibly, was recorded as receiving none.[37] Despite howls from the Fusionists, the legislature confirmed the results.

The aftermath of the election was even more telling. The Bourbon Democrats called for a constitutional convention and consolidated, for the time being, their power. Several provisions to restrict voting were written into the 1898 Constitution. The effects can be bluntly summarized: "between 1897 and 1904 white voter registration in Louisiana fell from almost 164,088 to 91,716, while black registration almost disappeared, zooming downward from 130,344 to 1,342."[38] In the spirit of Louisiana's disorderly political culture, to the victor went the spoils.

As in most of the American South, largely Celtic northern Europeans constitute a substantial part of Louisiana's political culture. But unlike in most of the remainder of the South, the position of these northern European traditionalists is not supreme in Louisiana, and the state's political culture reflects the existence of more influences. The southern Europeans, mainly French Acadians, add a second, very different point of view to the mix. Since neither the northern European nor the southern European culture is dominant, the whole culture of the state itself is unstable. Early on, by the turn of the twentieth century, Louisiana witnessed political turmoil as a result of this unstable culture.

The third group, African Americans, was allowed to participate in politics in any large-scale, systematic, enduring way only in the last fifty years. The addition of African Americans to the already unstable political culture of Louisiana allowed some openings to power unseen in other southern states where African Americans constituted a considerable numerical force. In Mississippi, Georgia, Alabama, and South Carolina, states where blacks are a politically important proportion of the population, the dominant group, northern European traditionalists, was virtually unchallenged in defining political norms. Louisiana provided a perfect opportunity for this newly empowered group to find some political voice. Political participation rates indicate that blacks in Louisiana are the most empowered group of blacks in any state in the United States. The power of this third politicocultural group in the late twentieth century intensified the existing political volatility. Therefore, one clear feature of Louisiana's democracy is instability and volatility resulting from the existence of three distinct politically conscious cultures.

Mouth of the South

To exacerbate the volatility of a political culture sprouting from three ethnic groups, the geography of Louisiana adds a further layer of instability. Louisiana's location on the Mississippi River and the state's richness of natural resources toss additional competitive interests and political possibilities into the mix.

The most visibly distinctive geographical feature of Louisiana is that the state is located where the largest river in the country meets the sea. The river strengthened the agrarian and urban economies within Louisiana. By 1860, Louisiana was the most affluent agrarian state in the United States. In 1840, New Orleans was the fourth-largest city in the nation and a leading exporter.[39] Its situation around the Gulf outlets of the Mississippi River provides Louisiana with a delta of rich alluvial soil that supported the development of a plantation economy based on rice, sugar, and cotton. Affluent planters established large slaveholding plantations in the delta, particularly in the southeastern part of the state. Although the plantation crops shifted from sugar and rice to cotton as one traveled up the Mississippi, the plantation system extended throughout the delta from the southern to the northern part of the state, crosscutting the ethnic cleavages between Anglo-Americans in the north and French, Spanish, and Creoles in the south. However, the farther one travels from the river, the sparser plantations become. Thus the plantation system established an agrarian elite not solidly identifiable with any single ethnic group or region of the state.

In the nineteenth century, when commerce was dominated by water transport, the river also provided the state with a vast commercial bounty. The intersection of the sea and the water highway to much of the nation's interior created a bustling Old World commercial crossroad, New Orleans—the largest and most prominent city in Louisiana and indeed the single best-known feature of the state. In the early 1800s, New Orleans had become the largest city in the South and the second-largest port in America, behind New York City. New Orleans had a population that was growing rapidly and therefore changing in character constantly. The New Orleans commercial mentality was quite different from the plantation culture that prevailed in much of the rest of the state and the South.

Raymond Strother, a highly successful national Democratic strategist with deep political roots in Louisiana, once described New Orleans as "a whole 'nother country." He was right.[40] But if New Orleans is "a whole 'nother country," it is in a state full of whole 'nother countries. In other states, when a major city stands apart, politics is always divided in terms of the city versus the rest of the state. The terms are very familiar. In Illinois, the phrase that describes the state political divide is "Chicago and downstate"; in New York, it is "New York City and upstate."

In Louisiana, however, the impact of New Orleans on the state's political culture is mainly to reinforce and accentuate the already unstable nature of that culture. New Orleans does not tear the state into parts because the state was never together to begin with. The city only adds spice to an already boiling pot.

The Fuel of Competition . . .

Discovered in the early part of the twentieth century, oil and natural gas came to dominate and lubricate Louisiana politics, encouraging and exaggerating trends of populism and corruption. Like many a third-world backwater or banana republic, Louisiana for much of the twentieth century was a one-crop economy that allowed the government to provide the undereducated and impoverished population with basic needs. The abundant supply of oil and gas has had complicated effects. While it allowed the state to collect taxes from a prosperous industry, it also encouraged state politicians to be beholden to powerful interest groups. Although Texas, Oklahoma, and Alaska also had huge reserves of oil and gas, these revenue sources did not dominate their budgets and therefore their political cultures to the same extent as in Louisiana. While oil and gas extraction—as well as a rapidly growing petrochemical industry—provided well-paying jobs for a state that needed them, these jobs did not require much formal education and, therefore, education was not a high priority for state politicians. The long-term results were stunted economic development and a customary view of higher education as a luxury rather than a necessity.

An oil-and-gas-based economy was perfectly conducive to populist politics. The financially robust industry provided the money to the government through taxes; citizens working in blue-collar jobs that required only a basic education were, therefore, highly inclined to respond to a populist rhetoric of distributive politics. Populist policy was a policy of roads, bridges, and chickens in every pot. A populist education system provided the very basics for many rather than better things for the few. Free schoolbooks, free transportation to public schools, and a source of cheap, basic college education near everyone were signature programs.

All of this had an impact upon a political culture that was already volatile and fiercely, ruthlessly competitive. Huey Long was able to become the most powerful politician in the history of Louisiana, or perhaps any state, because of the combination of an existing political culture and the new opportunities provided by the petroleum industry. "Big Oil" provided rhetorical ammunition; it became the perfect, easy-to-understand "enemy of the people." It was a simple target that made a populist message resonate.

Oil and gas probably played an even more significant role in providing Louisiana (and its politicians) a tremendous source of tax revenue. Any populist politician at that moment could not only make promises to poor, frustrated rural white people, but could deliver on these promises. With the influx of oil and gas severance taxes into the state's budget, there was no need to tax the people, and politicians could behave like Santa Claus. For the average citizen it was the politics of representation without taxation. The ruthless culture was already in place; oil and gas gave Huey Long not only the perfect rhetorical enemy but also the money to come through with roads, bridges, free textbooks, and a wild assortment of other populist goodies.[41]

The money that the oil and gas paid to the government may also have had the effect of strengthening racial tolerance in Louisiana. It allowed Huey Long, as it would have allowed any populist at the time, to build a power base among poorer whites. It also allowed him to distribute goods fairly freely and consistently without requiring any individual sacrifices.

This situation allowed Long to appeal solely to the economic, rather than the cultural, aspect of populist rhetoric and, therefore, not resort to racism. In bad economic times, his counterparts, notably Theodore Bilbo in Mississippi and, after a racist conversion, Tom Watson in Georgia, used racism to cement their charismatic hold on the newly politically empowered white former sharecroppers. Two factors in Long's background mitigated against this tactic. Racist rhetoric may well have been uncomfortable for the son and grandson of men who had favored the Union cause over the Confederate. Perhaps more significantly, Long was raised in Winn Parish, which opposed secession before the Civil War and was a bastion of anti-Confederate sentiment during it, provided a Louisiana powerhouse for Populist Party strength in the 1890s, and fostered a burgeoning socialist movement in the early 1900s. The class warfare, the demonizing of big business and corporate interests, the uses of government to legitimately coerce redistribution of wealth were all natural parts of his political consciousness. He was therefore more convincing perhaps because, especially at first, he may have been more genuine than many populist politicians of the day in his claimed desire to take from the rich and give to the poor.[42]

The hard-nosed winner-take-all competition that characterized Longism was in part a result of the natural resource base of the state. Without oil and gas money, the political game would not be nearly as feasible or effective.

. . . and Corruption

The abundance of oil and gas in the state may also help explain the reputation for corruption in Louisiana politics: money has been known to encourage politicians to stray from ethical purity. After all, Longism is not known only for its share-the-wealth programs. Both Huey Long's and Earl Long's reputations for fostering corruption in politics in many ways overshadow the populist politics and programs that dominated their rhetoric.

Corruption surely existed before the discovery of oil and gas in Louisiana. Native Virginian David Boyd, who served as president of Louisiana State University during Reconstruction, claimed in 1874 that Louisianians "look upon the public as a sheep to be shorn, and office as the special fleece. Here, you know, a man who does not make all he can out of his official place is set down as a fool, or poor business manager."[43] But the vast sums of money provided by the new industry afforded the opportunity for government officials to extend this approach to office. Since they could spend on public works programs and services without having to tax individuals, the potential for corruption was enormous. Politicians could spend and spend and spend without any sense of accountability for the way the money was spent because it was not perceived as the people's money.

In this environment, if a brother-in-law or wealthy contributor made large sums of money when a bridge was built or a health service was provided because the state paid exorbitant prices, the average citizen could easily be lulled into just enjoying the benefits without worrying about the money wasted. After all, it was Texaco's money or Standard Oil's money that was being spent. One of the more notoriously flagrant examples of this attitude was that of Governor Dick Leche (1936–1939) who reportedly said, "When I took the oath of office, I didn't take any vows of poverty"—and was later imprisoned for a variety of crimes that involved stealing money from the state.[44] Leche is one of the better known of a long string of corrupt Louisiana politicians because he was caught and paid dearly for his crimes. In much of the twentieth century, Louisiana politicians indeed had the ability to be Santa Claus. They could give gifts to their citizens at what seemed to be no cost. In the process, they often seized upon the opportunity to be even more generous to themselves. Corruption was the almost inevitable result.

Dependence on a single industry like oil and gas may also have led to unethical politics in another way as well. Elected officials were so beholden to the industry for severance taxes and jobs that its lobbyists regularly engineered passage of regulations very favorable to corporate interests. By the end of the century environmentalists would decry the "deals with the devil" that secured the benefits of jobs and money at the expense of compromising the integrity of the water and air in the state.

The legacy of abundant natural resources in Louisiana certainly adds a substantial dimension to the Louisiana political culture in the twentieth century. The revenue that it generated, coupled with an already volatile political culture, created a context that allowed for the emergence of Huey Long and his brand of populism. Long-style populism set the stage for a form of politics in Louisiana that would last well after his death. Huey's brother Earl Long was the obvious heir to the Long tradition. As lieutenant governor to Richard Leche, he became acting governor when the scandal-ridden Leche resigned in 1939, and he was elected governor outright in 1948 and again in 1956.

Since Earl's day, an embarrassing parade of elected officials have been indicted or convicted, of whom the most notorious is four-term governor Edwin Edwards, elected in 1971, 1975, 1983, and 1991. Edwards was the most instrumental in keeping the Louisiana traditions of populism and corruption alive throughout the last quarter of the twentieth century. After surviving two trials for racketeering that ended in a hung jury and an acquittal during his third term, Edwards returned five years later to serve an unprecedented fourth term with his victory over David Duke.

Tyler Bridges, in his book about Edwards and the history of gambling in Louisiana, *Bad Bet on the Bayou*, summed up his gubernatorial career: "Some called him the 'Last Great American Populist.' Others knew him as the 'Cajun King.' Still others called him the 'Silver Zipper.' . . . He had first moved into the Governor's Mansion in 1971, and for the next twenty-five years, he flaunted his fondness for easy cash, pretty women, and high-stakes gambling as he dominated Louisiana's politics and used his razor-sharp mind and catlike reflexes to stay one step ahead of the law."[45]

Someone once asked Edwards, "Who is the best politician you ever saw? The governor smiled and answered, "Every day when I look in the mirror . . ."[46]

Edwards may be the best-known Louisiana politician since the Longs to have been embroiled in scandal, but he is certainly not the only one. The last three state commissioners of insurance were indicted and convicted of crimes. Various other statewide officials and legislators have, all after the Long era, been indicted for, and not infrequently convicted of, a wide array of misdeeds.

But is Louisiana the most politically corrupt state in the United States? Surely other states have their own corruption problems. The answer to the question depends, of course, on how corruption is measured. In a "corruption index," is a convicted statewide-elected insurance commissioner worth the same number of "corruption points" as, say, three convicted state representatives? What if the insurance commissioner was convicted in two states? What if the insurance commissioner was part of a steady stream of indicted insurance commissioners? Does consistency count? The measurement problem notwithstanding, it is fair to state that if Louisiana is not the most corrupt state in the nation, it is certainly in the major leagues. In 1949 the noted political scientist V. O. Key called Louisiana's corruption history in the early twentieth century "a record unparalleled in our times."[47] As the narrator of the splendid 1991 documentary *Louisiana Boys: Raised on Politics* says, "If you were a politician and wanted to put another state on the other side of the confessional booth, it would be Louisiana."[48]

The long, Long legacy of a populist political culture enabled by an oil-and-petrochemical economy may not easily fade, but the economy itself has changed dramatically in recent years. In 1982 fully 41 percent of Louisiana's revenue was energy-based; a decade later, that number had dropped to only 13 percent.[49] Considering that the natural resource base in Louisiana explains much of Louisiana politics during the last hundred years, this fundamental change in economic structure may well produce a change in this aspect of the state's politics. After a few decades of functioning in this new economic context, Louisiana may simply no longer have the money to be a populist, and potentially very corrupt, state.

Constitutions and More Constitutions

For evidence of a direct impact of a volatile political culture on concrete politics, one only needs to look at the constitutional history of Louisiana. Constitutions are supposed to be the basic fundamental laws that govern governments. They represent a set of accepted principles that create the arena for political conflict. If Louisiana political history is any indication, those fundamental principles themselves are the subject of political conflict.

Louisianians cannot seem to agree on a constitution for very long—and when they did, from 1921 to 1973, they changed the constitution so many times that not only was the stability of the rules in question, but after so many amendments amending amendments, the rules themselves probably were not even understood. The superlatives are quite telling. Louisiana has had eleven constitutions, more than any other state in the union. It has also had the longest constitution in the history of the United States. In 1973, when the present Louisiana constitution was written, the 1921 constitution had 526 amendments of the over 800 that were on placed on the state ballot for citizen approval. Louisiana constitutional history is the unstable backbone of its unstable political culture.

It May Be a Gumbo After All

Gus Weill is a prominent raconteur of Louisiana politics. He is a working campaign consultant, a television host and political commentator, and a published playwright. His political wisdom is more a wisdom of experience and insight than of charts, graphs, and the latest statistical techniques (although he may well know them). It is poetic wisdom. He describes the uniqueness of Louisiana politics metaphorically, as a poet would: "Louisiana politics is probably perceived to be different because our state is different. We inhabit here the darndest melting pot of almost any other state and our politics is a hodgepodge, this—if you'll excuse me—this gumbo of all these ingredients is almost a concoction of a mad scientist and was bound to produce something unique."[50]

Weill's intuition is sound. Louisiana politics *is* a gumbo. And there is beauty in the metaphor. Gumbo is an African word (for okra) appropriated by the French Acadians for a signature Louisiana dish that has made lots of money for the restaurants in big-city commercial New Orleans. But Louisiana's political culture is not just any mix of disparate ingredients. It is the peculiarity of the concoction—the ingredients, the proportions, and the cooking vessel itself (to stretch the metaphor much more than it should be stretched)—that explains the politics.

While Louisiana is best known as a southern state and as the home of New Orleans, those two features are only the beginning of the story. Louisiana is also a state whose culture is defined by three very distinct and conspicuous ethnic groups. North Louisiana is home to a rural American South culture. South Louisiana contains a French Acadian culture. African Americans are found throughout most of the state. All three coexist and are aware of the others' presence. All three are also aware that none dominates. It is a constantly unstable political culture. The "gumbo" is a particular kind of gumbo. It is a tripartite gumbo that never fully blends and whose only consistency is instability. In the twentieth century, the blend became more unstable because of the infusion of oil and gas severance taxes. Populist politics confronted the elite politics of the nineteenth century and the stakes were raised. Populist rhetoric raised expectations for goods and services, and therefore political conflict was about more, more, and more government spending. The fact that the revenue was not the result of direct sacrifices by most citizens created a political climate ripe for corruption as well. Politicians could spend money wastefully and even fraudulently and not be held particularly accountable by a public that was not taxed for that revenue. Fundamentally, Louisiana's political culture is characterized by volatility and disorder because of immigration patterns and geography. And because of the economics of its natural resource base, in the twentieth century, it was defined by populism and corruption as well.

2. Participation

"Politics Is the Favorite Sport"

Louisianians often talk about how they love politics. "Politics is the favorite sport down here" and "Politics is entertainment in Louisiana" are phrases that have been heard thousands of times in thousands of discussions of politics in Louisiana. According to this front-porch logic, Louisianians engage in politics more enthusiastically and vote more often than folks in any part of the country. In a state where no ethnic group dominates, where the three main ethnic groups do not trust each other, and where all are constantly maneuvering for position, there is ample motivation for stormy wide-open elections. In addition, for most of the twentieth century the state was flush with oil and gas money that could grease the wheels of campaigns. The resources were clearly there for constant, high-risk, high-return appeals to the people. This cultural combination of immigration patterns and abundant valuable resources seems like the perfect foundation for a highly participatory politics. The culture predicts it and the people believe it, but does Louisiana actually deserve bragging rights for political participation? The answer is no—and yes.

No matter how much crawfish and beer skeptical social scientists have consumed, they are quick to point out that Louisianians do not vote more than citizens of other states. In fact, in most national elections, Montana, South Dakota, and Maine top the turnout lists and Louisiana is near the national average. In the 2000 presidential election, voter turnout in Louisiana was 54 percent and ranked twenty-second in the nation. Minnesota, Maine and Wisconsin topped the list with over 65 percent turnout.

Among southern states, however, Louisiana fares much better. In fact, Louisiana ranked higher than any of the eleven states of the old Confederacy. Turnout in Mississippi was 49 percent, in Georgia it was 43 percent, in Alabama it was 50 percent, in Arkansas it was 48 percent, and in South Carolina it was 46 percent. In sum, in the 2000 presidential election Louisiana ranked well above the southern average in voter turnout, but only slightly above the national average. See table 2-A

(Appendix 2) for the complete results.

The 2000 election is not an isolated case. A well-known academic index of turnout in presidential, gubernatorial, and U.S. Senate and House elections in the 1990s reinforces the 2000 results. (See table 2-B.) Average turnout in Louisiana was 46.1 percent, almost exactly the national average, although again well above all of the states in the South.

As is often the case, the legend, the conventional wisdom, the front-porch logic is grounded in some truth. Stark, simple voter turnout statistics can be misleading. Upon closer inspection, while Louisiana may not be the most participatory state in the United States by these measures, it is abnormally participatory by other criteria. All of the states of the South have lower voter participation levels; indeed, all are normally in the bottom half of the voter turnout statistics. Southern states are disproportionately poorer and less educated, and voting is clearly associated with higher education and higher income; therefore, southern states have lower turnout. One common explanation for this phenomenon is that the physical costs of voting are higher for poorer people. It is more difficult to get transportation to the polls and often more difficult to find the time for it.

Therefore, for a relatively poor, less-educated state, Louisiana has unusually participatory voters. Indeed, if elections for the U.S. House of Representatives, where Louisiana incumbents have an astonishingly high rate of running without opposition, are not considered, Louisiana would rise firmly into the top half of state turnout and would be easily the most participatory state among those with less-educated and lower-income populations.

Elections for Everything: "We need someone to sue us"

Voter turnout is the simplest, but not the only, indicator of a participatory culture. The foremost distinction in Louisiana political participation is on the supply side of the ledger. In this volatile, unstable political culture where political power is always tentative, Louisiana's numerous elections are a clear earmark of a culture of competition. The state's appetite for elections and campaigns seems insatiable. Louisiana holds elections for almost everything—even the commissioner of elections. Statewide elections are taken very seriously. Louisiana is one of only five states to hold state elections in off-years, a clear indicator of the desire to separate national politics from state politics (Virginia and New Jersey hold elections the year after a presidential election; Mississippi, Kentucky, and Louisiana, the year before). Louisiana elections also have a history of bulging campaign war chests for runs at every office from governor to city council.

The election of the commissioner of elections is the most notorious instance of the Louisiana political culture's making a bureaucratic function political and elective. The office that is designed to regulate elections is itself elected because of a shameless political move. In 1956 Governor Earl Long was displeased that his political enemy Wade O. Martin Jr. had been elected secretary of state. Worse, Martin hinted that he might be a candidate for governor—and he had a firm power base from which to challenge Long.[1] Louisiana's secretary of state had constitutional control over the lucrative voting machine contract, the politically rewarding certification of voting commissioners, and regulation of the politically and financially valuable insurance business, as well as the promulgation of the election results. Long brazenly and successfully stripped Martin of his most politically beneficial administrative duties. The governor convinced the legislature to create a statewide-elected insurance commissioner and unabashedly created a statewide-elected commissioner of elections with authority over voting machine purchases and certification of voting commissioners. The effect of these actions was obvious and the atmosphere at the legislature was rambunctious: "At a committee hearing, Martin and Long shouted insults at each other, nearly came to blows when they wrestled over a microphone, and both had to be restrained. In the end, stripped of these functions, Martin would be reduced to certifying election returns, swearing in public officials, administering the state archives, and other politically insignificant functions."[2] At the end of the day, Louisiana had two more officials elected statewide. Despite the turbulent and outrageous genesis of these two offices, they remained in the next Louisiana constitution, drafted in 1974. Provisions were made in that constitution for legislative prerogative to make the offices appointive again—in case the politics of some future day warranted a change.[3]

The election of a commissioner of elections is part of a pattern in Louisiana. While governor is the only office that all fifty states elect, a majority of the states, including Louisiana, also elect a lieutenant governor, attorney general, state treasurer, and secretary of state.[4] Louisiana joins very few states that elect much more. Unlike most other states, Louisiana also elects an agriculture commission (seven other states), public service commissioners (eight other states), insurance commissioner (seven other states), and, of course, Louisiana is the only state that has ever elected an election commissioner. Like all other states, Louisiana elects the members of the legislative branch—the house of representatives and the senate—but it elects all of its judges as well. So while legislative elections in the fifty states mirror the national government, Louisiana joins a small minority of states that use the electoral process to select a preponderance of the major statewide executive offices and an even smaller minority whose judicial branch is made up of members chosen via elections. The variations in state judicial selection are shown in table 2-C in Appendix 2.

The tenacity with which Louisiana politics holds onto the electoral process is exemplified in the state's historic reaction to the problem of a lack of African American judges in all levels of state courts. Even though roughly one-third of Louisiana's population is African American, only a handful of the hundreds of district court judges, court of appeals judges, or supreme court judges elected in Louisiana have been black. Until the federal courts intervened, judicial voting districts were made up of either a whole parish or multiple parishes, and since only Orleans Parish was a majority black jurisdiction, almost all judges outside Orleans were white (Louisiana votes along fairly stark and predictable racial lines). The federal courts required that Louisiana change its judicial selection system in a way that more black judges could be selected. A simple solution to this problem would have been to adopt a policy used by most other states. Long before the issue became one that required court intervention, Louisiana could have abandoned the practice of electing all judges and moved to a system that included appointment as part of the process for at least some judges. When it finally came to the attention of the courts in 1991, several decades after ending racial discrimination had became a national priority, the federal judge was unwilling to accept that remedy.[5] Because of these sorts of issues, Louisiana is commonly forced to redraw district lines and hold special elections—often at tremendous financial cost to the state. In this instance, Louisiana was in a such a precarious situation that, in August 1991, First Assistant Secretary of State Bob Courtney proclaimed, "We need someone to sue us."[6] The United States Federal District Court presented a consent decree that dictated how judges were to be elected in Louisiana. As a result, many judges who have jurisdiction over an entire parish or a set of parishes are elected from a subdistrict within the parish. While this cumbersome situation of adjudication without representation may cause some political science theorists to wince, it is consistent with the tradition of a state where elections are such a fundamental part of the culture.

More Money Than the Louisiana Purchase

You can almost measure the strength of the economy in Louisiana by the number of yard signs littering the state during an election. When Louisianians have the money, they spend exorbitant amounts on campaigns. When conditions are right, few states compare to Louisiana in campaign spending. In fact, in 1983, when the state was still enjoying the fruits of the oil boom, more money was spent on a governor's race in Louisiana than in any nonpresidential race in American history up until that time. At the height of the Louisiana oil-boom wealth, political campaigns in Louisiana routinely rivaled and eclipsed those in much larger and more populous states. Big contributors had money to spend on politics. However, when the economy wanes, so does campaign spending.

The 1983 governor's race that broke the spending records was between incumbent Republican Dave Treen and former two-term Democratic governor Edwin Edwards. It promised to be an entertaining affair because of the challenge from Edwards, who was not only extremely colorful but had been enormously popular when he finished the second of his two constitutionally allowed consecutive terms in 1979. Treen had a much more businesslike demeanor and found himself in the unfortunate circumstance of having lowered taxes only to see the bottom fall out of state oil and gas revenue when the price of oil dropped on international markets. Edwards was favored to defeat the incumbent and appeared to relish the chance—he obviously wanted to enjoy the experience. In the end, Edwards won handily and over $20 million had been spent on the election. The victory was accentuated by a multimillion-dollar fundraising jaunt to Paris. Edwards's brother Marion, who organized the trip, said, "By the time this trip is over, I will have raised more than what Jefferson paid for Louisiana in 1803."[7] He was right. Thomas Jefferson had paid $15 million for the entire Louisiana Purchase. Marion Edwards raised 13 million for the campaign and 4 million to repay letters of credit.[8] Neither Louisiana nor the nation had ever seen anything like it.

The notorious 1983 election for governor was the subject of a book by the prominent Louisiana political columnist John Maginnis. The book was astutely titled *The Last Hayride* because the election appears to have marked the (temporary?) end of an era in which Louisiana had the resources to go with the desire to win the latest round.

Few things better illustrate the connection between culture and politics than Louisiana's history of campaign spending. The state's ethnic mix would predict heavy competition for every office; the oil and gas wealth allows spending in the elections to go through the roof. When both are evident, buckets of money are spent in Louisiana campaigns. As political consultant Ray Strother sums it up, "I've seen people spend more money running for city council of New Orleans than running for governor of Connecticut. I actually ran a campaign for the governor of Connecticut, Bill O'Neal, where we spent less than a million dollars. I've seen more than a million dollars spent in so many races. Here there's a little tiny town outside of New Orleans called Kenner, I don't know how many tens of millions of dollars have been spent there. It's just phenomenal!"[9]

A Primary without a Party

Few things confound outsiders who try to understand Louisiana politics more than Louisiana's bizarre election system. When America's Founding Fathers decided that elections were properly the domain of states rather than the national government, they might have hesitated a bit more if they had thought that states would be as willing as Louisiana to experiment with the rules of democracy.

States are normally broken down into categories that are defined by the way the voters choose the party nominee who will have a place in the general election. Seventeen states limit the selection of a party nominee to citizens who are registered party members. The remaining thirty-six states, all but Louisiana, chose among a variety of rules that allow citizens to select which party primary to vote in on election day and even, in some cases, to vote in different party primaries for different offices. In all of these forty-nine normal states, however, voters are selecting a party nominee for each office. (See table 2-D, Appendix 2.)

Every normal state has an election system in which each of the two main parties has a nominee in the general election. Louisiana does not. The Louisiana election system is not only abnormal, showing total disregard for the notion of party government, but it has already been found unconstitutional for a completely different reason and is probably on shaky ground in a couple of other ways.

When Louisiana's current system was proposed, good-government groups and academicians howled. Practically every legislative session brings a serious attempt to change the election rules to resemble those of the forty-nine other states. Despite all the criticism, Louisiana's system has not only weathered more than a quarter of a century of politics, it has produced some of our more memorable elections. In addition, in the last decade, some of the at least nominally normal states—for example, Washington and California—have modified their systems in ways that make them more like Louisiana's.

The origins of our present election law are a classic Louisiana story rooted in the growing pains of the two-party system and the political brazenness of Governor Edwin Edwards. In the early 1970s, the rise of the Republican Party in the South was beginning to ripple in Louisiana as well. As early as 1956, Dwight D. Eisenhower had become the first Republican presidential candidate to carry the state, and in 1964 Republican Barry Goldwater's socially conservative message had a dramatic impact on the state's politics. The trickle down to state political office was slow but definite—and certainly not lost on the more astute Democratic candidates. Few politicians were more astute than Edwin Edwards, who saw a political problem and acted to change it.

Before 1975, Louisiana had used the same election system as most southern states: Citizens and candidates registered by party, all registered party members voted in a party primary for the party nominee. If one candidate received a majority, that candidate would run under the party label in the general election. If no candidate received a majority, the top two candidates would participate in a runoff and the winner of the runoff would be the party nominee in the general election.

This was a particularly southern way of conducting elections, one that developed out of the racial voting patterns in the South. If, for instance, the biggest vote total in a Democratic primary for governor was for an African American candidate who received 30 percent of the votes, that candidate would be the party nominee under the no-runoff rules in many places outside the South. Inside the South, however, that candidate would be thrown into a runoff with the next-highest vote getter—most likely a white candidate, who would win easily in the runoff if normal racial voting patterns held. When almost all registered voters and candidates in Louisiana were Democrats, the Democratic primary served as the de facto election. The person who won the Democratic primary outright or who won the runoff almost invariably won the general election. Therefore, before 1975, conventional wisdom was that in order to participate meaningfully in choosing any significant elected official, it was necessary to register as Democrat and vote in the Democratic primary. Heated battles for the Democratic nomination were the heart of the democratic process in Louisiana.

The 1971 race for governor was not only a perfect example of a freewheeling, no-holds-barred, highly competitive Democratic primary that was tantamount to election, but it also provided the impetus for the change in election rules. John McKeithen had been easily reelected after convincing voters and the legislature to change the constitution to allow him to serve an unprecedented two consecutive terms as governor. Therefore, for the first time in Louisiana history, in 1971 voters had waited eight years to select a new political kingpin. The time was ripe for a colorful high-stakes political battle, and the candidates rose to the occasion. Congressman Edwin Edwards, whose campaign for governor was highly visible for over a year, was joined by prominent long-term congressman Gillis Long, six-term lieutenant governor C. C. "Taddy" Aycock, two-term former Governor Jimmie H. Davis, successful grocer and state senator John G. Schwegmann, well-regarded Shreveport state senator J. Bennett Johnston, and a host of lesser-known candidates.

The campaign was a spirited, well-funded series of debates, debacles, barbs, attacks, and responses with some discussion of issues. After a long, hard year of fundraising, speeches, traveling, polling, debating, producing ads, shaking hands, and kissing babies, Edwin Edwards, with 23 percent of the vote, and Bennett Johnston, with only 18 percent of the vote, emerged as the top two candidates in the initial Democratic primary. Since neither had achieved anything close to a majority, they were poised to meet in a hard-fought runoff for the Democratic nomination.

The runoff was itself a classic Louisiana contest—the closest governor's primary in Louisiana history. Edwards received 584,262 votes to 579,744 for Johnston. The breakdown of the vote demographically reveals that the battle lines of support were distinctly political, rather than based on personal image. Even a casual glance at the parish and precinct returns, combined with an informal look at endorsements, advertisements, and campaign travel, shows some obvious political support patterns. Edwards formed a potent coalition of African Americans, labor, and Catholics, while Johnston marshaled a formidable alliance of white Protestants and suburbanites. Both coalitions would prove to be durable ones. Edwards's supporters would later form the core of the state's voters for Democratic candidates for president, U.S. Senate, and governor, while the Johnston-supporter demographics would characterize voters for Republican candidates for those offices. Perhaps such a highly competitive, coalition-building race was fitting for a contest between two future Louisiana legends. Edwards would go on to serve a record-setting four terms as governor. Johnston would be elected to the United States Senate the next year and serve until his retirement in 1996.

In 1971, however, Edwards, having survived two draining elections against formidable opponents within the Democratic Party, still faced one more hurdle before he could call himself governor of Louisiana: a credible Republican candidate, Congressman Dave Treen. Although Treen was a distinct underdog, the Republican's campaign had some advantages over the Democrat's that did not go unnoticed by Edwards. The most obvious one was that, since there were so few Republican candidates, and rarely more than one candidate for major office, Republican primaries were normally not contested. The benefit to Treen, and by extension any viable Republican in major elections in the near future, was the lack of a bruising nomination fight. Surely many supporters of Edwards's Democratic opponents in the primary and runoff had accepted their candidates' negative portrayals of Edwards. Some of these disenchanted Democrats either stayed away from the polls or voted for Treen. In the general election, Edwards was a candidate who had been punched in the face several times by his opponents, whereas Treen had been generally ignored. Edwards won, but he would not forget this lesson.

Political scientists have debated whether a bitterly fought primary race helps or hurts the victor in the general election, but candidates like Edwards who have endured such battles understandably prefer a gentler road to the nomination. In a combative primary fight, not only is the candidate's ego bruised, but the heightened opportunity and need for negative campaigning may spur investigations into personal and private aspects of the candidate's life that would otherwise have gone unnoticed.

While candidates may successfully weather the storm and rely on the old axiom that all publicity is good publicity, and while social science studies may indicate that there may even be an advantage for the competitive primary winner over the nominee who had little primary opposition, Edwards thought otherwise. He focused on the extra money spent in his pursuit of the Democratic nomination, as well as on the great personal effort required to win three elections (primary, runoff, general election) instead of only a single general election and, at most, one runoff. Edwards's next step was to do what politicians in other states may only dream of doing: he changed the election system to suit him.

In order to win approval for a change, Edwards needed to sound less like an ambitious politician and more like a political philosopher, or at the very least, an election policy expert. He made a case for completely scrapping the party primary. Instead, all candidates, regardless of party affiliation, would compete in a single initial election, and if no one received a majority, the top two candidates, regardless of party affiliation, would participate in a runoff. If a candidate received a majority of votes in the initial election, that candidate would be declared the winner and no runoff would be necessary.

This approach was dubbed the "open primary system" and was quickly called that throughout the state by politicians and journalists alike. Unfortunately, in the rest of the nation, the term *open primary system* refers to something else—a partisan primary in which party registration is not required in order to vote in the primary. But the name stuck and confusion about Louisiana election law was only compounded in the forty-nine ordinary states.

Edwards argued that the new system would enhance democracy in Louisiana by making it easier for citizens to vote in the initial selection of candidates. Under the old system, only registered Democrats could vote in the Democratic primary and registered Republicans in the Republican primary. Since at that time a large majority of major candidates for almost every elective office, from governor and U.S. senator down to police juror, were Democrats, citizens who were not registered as Democrats could not participate in the initial winnowing of candidates. By stripping away party primaries altogether, anyone could participate in all parts of the election process (the selection of presidential nominees was the only exception to this rule). Edwards even argued that the new system would give some life to the budding Republican Party because the overwhelming number of registered Democrats in the state would be free to vote for Republicans, even in the initial election. In addition, Republican-leaning voters would have no fear of being left out of the crucial Democratic primary, since no exclusive party primary would exist under the new plan. Furthermore, the open election system would cut costs to both the government and candidates by reducing the number of elections from a maximum of three to a maximum of two, and it would enhance democracy by removing the closed partisan primary.

Opposition to the new system came mainly from good-government groups and academics—neither widely regarded as powerhouses in the rough-and-tumble world of Louisiana politics. Yet their reasoning was understandable. This Louisiana election system would remove any semblance of consistency with the electoral laws of the other forty-nine states by completely eradicating the concept of the party primary. Other states vary in the ways in which voters can participate in the party primary (open vs. closed) and the rules by which candidates are declared winners (majority vs. plurality), but all states hold party primaries. The inconsistency is more than symbolic. Among other things, it would mean that Louisiana is not guaranteed to be part of a single national election day on which the two parties' candidates square off against each other all over the country for seats in the U.S. Senate and House of Representatives. In Louisiana, the opponents on general election day might as easily be two Democrats or two Republicans. The system would also present the opportunity for a candidate to win a majority of the vote in the first election and not compete in a general national election day at all. It was this problem that eventually caused the United States Supreme Court to declare the system unconstitutional.

It was also this final characteristic—candidates could win outright in the first election—that made it so appealing to the legislators who were to decide its fate. Academics and good-government groups were no match for legislative incumbents who saw the opportunity to win reelection by competing in a single election. In addition, these mostly Democratic incumbents could avoid the possibility of having to fight a general election against an upstart Republican by simply winning a majority of the votes in the first election. In August 1975, only months before the next elections for governor, other statewide offices, and the entire legislature, the system was overwhelmingly voted into law and signed by the governor. That fall, Edwards and every statewide elected official won handily in the first election, and most legislative incumbents did the same. In the eyes of incumbent state officials, in the first actual elections under the new rules, the open election system had performed magnificently.

After two decades of Louisiana's using the rules, the federal courts finally took action and declared the process unconstitutional for reasons that seemed obvious the day they were first proposed. In 1997 the Supreme Court affirmed a U.S. District Court ruling that Louisiana must elect its members of the U.S. House of Representatives and Senate on the same day as the remaining states. The ruling, in a strange twist, suggested how the state could remedy the situation without fundamentally altering the rules. The Court said that Louisiana could move the date of the initial election to the national general election day, and if a runoff were necessary, hold it in a reasonable time after the initial election. This proposal was based on the fact that an overwhelming proportion of elections had been decided in that first phase when, typically, an incumbent would win more than the combined total of all challengers.

Oddly, this solution set up the distinct possibility that instead of electing members of Congress weeks before the national election day, Louisiana would now fairly often be electing them weeks after the national election day. The prospect of a Louisiana runoff deciding the partisan majority fate of an evenly divided House or Senate three or four weeks after the national general election probably whetted the appetites of Louisiana's political consultants, but it seemed to be dismissed by the courts.

In an era of slim majorities in both chambers of Congress, there is a real possibility that a single member of the U.S. Senate or House of Representatives could tip the balance of power in the government. If either chamber is evenly divided after national election day, a single runoff election weeks later in Louisiana could determine control of the Senate or the House. If those cases become more common, Louisianians had better get accustomed to seeing Tom Brokaw at the local Burger King in November and December of election years.

Regardless of the dates involved, numerous elections at all levels have already been executed under Louisiana's open primary system, and some of its broader implications can now be addressed. Did it help the Republicans as Edwards had argued it would? Some Republicans claim that the system did indeed make it easier for Louisiana voters to switch their allegiance from the Democratic Party to the Republican Party without having to make the effort of changing their voter registration. And new voters no longer had the incentive to register as Democrats because the closed Democratic primary, where most viable candidates usually ran, no longer existed. Other Republicans, however, contend that open primaries actually stunted the growth of the Republican Party: Since there were no longer Republican primaries and since people who were changing their party support had no practical reason to take the time and effort needed to actually change their party registration, party loyalty was not reinforced. These Republicans argue that the act of changing registration and voting in party primaries would increase the commitment of those thousands of Louisiana voters who during the seventies and eighties began to identify with the Republican Party.

John Maginnis, the best-known political commentator in the state, acknowledges that state and local party officials "loathe" the open primary system. He himself loves it: "The open primary is so simple, so direct, so of the people, that of course party leaders view it as dangerous. The beauty and terror of it are that it gives the people exactly what they ask for, without the filtering by political parties."[10] Maginnis admits that even his fellow pundits do not necessarily agree with him: "Outside commentators ridicule Louisiana's 'peculiar,' 'screwball,' even 'dangerous' election process, as though it were a French mutant perversion of the Magna Carta."[11]

The most common objection to open election centers not on the ramifications for parties themselves, but on the types of candidates who benefit and are harmed by the system. Problems in this regard are normally confined to elections in which no incumbent is running and the field draws several candidates from across the political spectrum. The concern was voiced by former congressman (and aspiring Speaker of the House) Robert Livingston, who asserted that "good solid candidates from the mainstream . . . get shunted out." Democratic and Republican party activists object to what they see as the propensity for the system to elect, in Livingston's term, "fringe" candidates.[12] In a state where colorful, brash, outspoken candidates are a normal part of the political landscape, that criticism is a strong one. For a candidate to be described as "fringe" in Louisiana is quite a statement. Several recent elections support the general notion that candidates on the edges of the ideological spectrum are likely to make it into the runoff, while moderate candidates from either party often find themselves splitting the middle-of-the-road vote and dropping out.

The 1986 election for the Eighth Congressional District provided the most outlandish example of the predicament that Livingston, a Republican, describes, although in this case it was the Democratic Party that suffered. Democrats lost in the "safely Democratic" sprawling Eighth District, which covered Alexandria in the middle of the state and ran south to the heavily unionized parishes north and west of Baton Rouge. The now defunct district was dominated by white union Democrats who had sent Gillis Long to Congress for years and who, in a special election after his death, chose his wife, Cathy, to fill out his term.

In 1986 Cathy decided not to run for election on her own, and the race attracted three candidates who seemed to be appropriate political and ideological heirs to the Long seat—moderate, white labor Democrats, all articulate and fairly well known in their respective parts of the sprawling district. The election also attracted a conservative Republican, Clyde Holloway, and a fairly liberal black Democrat, Faye Williams. Under a normal party primary system in this heavily Democratic district, a district that Democratic presidential hopeful Walter Mondale had carried in 1976, Holloway the Republican would likely have lost to the winner of the Democratic runoff. Given the racial voting patterns in the state, Williams would almost certainly have garnered enough support to make a runoff, but would then as certainly have lost to the top vote-getter among the three white Democratic candidates. Under the Louisiana system, however, with no party primaries, all five candidates ran together in a single election. To the dismay of Democratic Party regulars, Holloway and Williams made the runoff.

The runoff was fairly disconcerting for the majority of voters in the district, who were accustomed to voting for whites and Democrats. Now they had a choice between a black Democrat and a white Republican. The race was close, but racial and perhaps ideological loyalty eclipsed party loyalty, and Clyde Holloway became the only Republican elected to Congress from a district that Mondale had carried two years earlier. Louisiana election rules produce peculiar outcomes indeed.

While Democrats may have lost a congressional seat because of the dynamics of the election system, Republicans had to face an even more ominous consequence of the "fringe" effect a few years later—David Duke. Duke, the former Klansman who had gained political credibility by winning a special election to the state house of representatives from suburban New Orleans, became an albatross around the neck of Republican efforts in several important races. In 1990, Democratic U.S. senator Bennett Johnston was a key Republican target, and Republicans in Louisiana had reasonable hopes of unseating the three-term senator. Under a normal set of party primaries, a moderate Republican might well have emerged as the opposition. Instead, Duke emerged as the only major Republican opponent in the election, and prominent Republicans in Louisiana and across the country, including Republican president George Bush, found themselves in the incredibly embarrassing position of supporting the Democratic candidate.

Only one year later, Louisiana Republicans were unable to defeat their most despised nemesis, Governor Edwin Edwards, because Duke emerged as his runoff opposition. Edwards, whose popularity and reputation had waned greatly since his last stint as governor, should have been vulnerable. But in what must have seemed like a bad dream to Republican loyalists, in an election that received extraordinary national and international attention, Edwards received the reluctant support of many Republicans and won an unprecedented fourth term. The Louisiana election system had served Edwards well once more, and Louisiana politics had never seemed more volatile.

Almost every legislative session brings an attempt to change the election system. The proponents of the alternative rules invariably testify in committee hearings that their particular system is best for democracy, party government, voter participation, brotherhood, sisterhood, world peace, and anything else that sounds worthwhile. Equally predictable is the inevitable link between the particular proposal and the potential for good fortune for whatever party or political group or interest the legislator represents. After all, the election system itself is a product of incumbent legislators wanting to boost their reelection prospects. Therefore, any knowing Louisiana politician ignores the democracy talk and tries to figure out exactly how any proposed change in the system will help him or her. In the last twenty-five years bluffs have been called, political points have been made, and the odd, eccentric election system remains a fitting testament to the uniqueness of the Louisiana culture.

Sort of Southern . . .

Voting patterns in Louisiana have never been easy for outsiders to understand. Analysts find it tempting to lazily lump Louisiana in with the other Deep South states and explain its voting patterns in southern terms. However, Louisiana voters are southern voters with some complications. As mentioned earlier, in the most legendary and defining event in southern history, secession from the Union and Civil War, Louisiana was not a completely straightforward participant. Charles Dew's characterization of Louisiana as the Deep South state least likely to secede from the Union seems solid.[13]

Louisiana did of course secede, and Louisiana is most certainly a southern state. But its voting patterns are often more like states outside the South. In fact, Louisiana has been the most "American" of the southern states in the last thirty years. Louisiana is the only one of the eleven states of the old Confederacy to have voted for the national winner in every presidential election since 1972. In 1992 it was the only state other than Bill Clinton's home state of Arkansas and his running mate Al Gore's home state of Tennessee to vote Democratic. Not Florida, not Virginia, not Texas, not Tennessee but Louisiana has had the most nonsouthern, most American voting patterns in the last thirty years. In Louisiana's complicated political culture, "southern" north Louisianians and rural African Americans exhibit vote choices and turnout statistics much like those of their counterparts in the remainder of the South. South Louisiana and New Orleans voters, however, stray from the Dixie norm. Louisiana is a peculiar state in a peculiar region. Attempts to understand Louisiana voting patterns as simply the voting patterns of a state in the Deep South will often lead to mistakes and misunderstandings and inaccurate predictions.

The comparison and contrast to Mississippi is revealing. Mississippi is similar to Louisiana in several important political characteristics. Both have a strong one-party Democratic history that started with the end of the Civil War and lasted until the late twentieth century. The two states have the two highest percentages of African Americans in the nation, and African Americans are among the most politically cohesive groups in the nation. Both states are among the lowest in most measures of income and education. These four characteristics—partisanship history, race, income, and education—are the standard predictors of how states vote. Louisiana and Mississippi are virtually identical on all four. And in state politics, the two states look a lot alike. In both states the state senate and house of representatives have comfortable Democratic majorities, in both states most of the statewide elected officials are Democrats, and in both states Republicans have been successful in electing and reelecting the top of the ticket, the governor.

In national politics, however, there are striking differences. In national politics, Republicans seem to dominate in Mississippi, while Democrats appear to be much more competitive in Louisiana. Louisiana's two U.S. senators are Democrats; Mississippi's two are Republicans. In the last three presidential elections, Mississippi has voted Republican all three times, while Louisiana has voted Democratic twice. In fact, in 1992, Mississippi gave President Bush his highest vote percentage in the nation, while Governor Clinton won by 12 percentage points in Louisiana. In recent presidential elections, Mississippi is usually ceded by both parties to the Republicans, and therefore neither Democratic nor Republican presidential campaigns spend much time or resources in that state. Louisiana, on the other hand, is tightly contested and receives a wealth of candidate visits and advertising. In fact, in a study of the strategies of the 1996 presidential campaigns, Louisiana was one of only three states that both the Democrats and Republicans targeted for disproportionate attention (Nevada and New Mexico were the others).[14] Mississippi was written off completely by the Democrats in both cases.

In state politics, both Louisiana and Mississippi are competitive for statewide office and mostly Democratic in local and regional elections. In national politics, Mississippi is a solid Republican state and Louisiana is a competitive state. In short, Louisiana is both southern like Mississippi and not southern.

The second half of the twentieth century produced a partisan revolution in the South and in Louisiana. Indeed, the South was the home of the most dramatic voting changes in all of American politics in the twentieth century. The significance of the up-for-grabs party dynamics of the South to national politics is a fact so obvious that it's almost forgotten, but the evidence is clear. Four of the last six elected presidents (counting Clinton twice) were from southern states, the leadership of the Republican Party is dominated by southerners, and the historic 1994 sweep of Republicans to a majority in the House of Representatives was an overwhelmingly southern phenomenon. These phenomena reflect the evolution of the

South from a region of staggering one-party Democratic dominance to a competitive two-party system where, in elections for national office, Republicans hold a clear edge. This Republican revolution occurred in Louisiana as well, because much of the Louisiana culture is southern.

The changes over time in the simple numbers of Democratic and Republican victories in the region are stunning. At the end of World War II, roughly a century after the Civil War, no Republican presidential candidate had carried a single state in the Deep South, and with only minor exceptions, Democratic presidential candidates had won every election in the entire region. At that time only two or three of the roughly 125 congressmen from the region were Republicans; the remainder were all Democrats. And amazingly, as of 1960 not a single one of the eleven states that seceded from the Union had even once popularly elected a Republican to the United States Senate. The South was truly a one-party, solidly Democratic region. Yet by 1994, Republicans had gained so much strength that for the first time in history, Republicans were elected to a majority of seats from the South in both houses of Congress. Republicans captured 64 of 125 southern seats in the House of Representatives and held 12 of 22 southern seats in the Senate. (The next year two Louisiana Democratic members of the House of Representatives, W. J. "Billy" Tauzin and Jimmy Hayes, switched parties and became Republicans—giving Louisiana a majority Republican delegation to Congress.) In addition, between 1964 and 2000, Republican presidential candidates carried most of the eleven states more often than Democrats did. Most strikingly, in the highly competitive 2000 presidential election, all eleven states in the South voted Republican—a solid Republican South.

While Louisiana may not have been the heart of the Republican revolution in the South and may not have experienced the revolution as profoundly as Mississippi or Alabama, Louisiana may have played a role in the genesis of it. In 1939 a graduate student from Minnesota, Hubert H. Humphrey, traveled to Louisiana to study the populist politics of Huey Long. He enrolled in the master's degree program in Political Science at Louisiana State University and quickly became an outstanding student. It was his social life in Baton Rouge, rather than his studies, that had a deep-felt impact on his politics and, by extension, American and southern politics. He had a firsthand look at race relations in the South and was appalled.[15] The racial discrimination and racial apartheid in Baton Rouge affected him so much that civil rights and voting rights for blacks became a main focus of his political agenda when he returned to Minnesota and began a stellar political career first as mayor of Minneapolis, then Minnesota United States senator, and eventually vice president under Lyndon Johnson. When he stirred the Democratic National Convention with a passionate speech favoring a strong civil rights platform in 1948, Humphrey helped transform party politics in America, and particularly in the South.

The speech effectively roused enough delegates to give the civil rights plank a 243-234 victory. When it passed, several southern Democratic delegates walked out of the convention. They later formed their own alternative to the Democratic ticket, with Strom Thurmond as their States' Rights Party presidential candidate. This "Dixiecrat" revolt, as it was characterized in the popular press, was the beginning of the end of Democratic dominance in the South.

While the 1948 Democratic Convention signaled the end of Democratic dominance among the white majority in the South, it also marked the beginning of Democratic Party commitment among blacks, who at the time were largely disfranchised in the southern states. Clearly the issue of civil rights for blacks was the catalyst for the break with the dominant party among whites. White Democratic resistance to black rights in the twentieth-century South had been so strong that it practically defined the party. In fact, the Supreme Court's 1944 decision overturning white-only Democratic primaries convinced white southern segregationists that their values were being severely threatened and attacked by the nation's major political institutions. It was this atmosphere of panic among white segregationists that allowed dramatic upheavals in the party structure.

While the rise of the Republican Party in the South was not born of racial segregationism, the hegemony of the Democratic Party in the region died because of the party's commitment to the race issue. Blacks, who constituted about a third of potential voters in the Deep South, found themselves changing their allegiance from the party of Lincoln, the Republican Party, to the party of Hubert Humphrey because of the strong stand of the Democratic Party on civil rights. Black loyalty to the Democratic Party eventually became one of the key, enduring, stable elements of the southern party system. White segregationists who left the

Democratic Party briefly in 1948 did not find a comfortable home in the Republican Party during the next decade, as both parties tried to appear moderate on the race issue in their 1952 and 1956 conventions. In 1964, however, everything changed. Democratic presidential candidate Lyndon Johnson had selected civil rights champion Hubert Humphrey as his running mate, and Republican presidential nominee Barry Goldwater campaigned on a states' rights platform and rejected the need for a Civil Rights Act and Voting Rights Act. The effect on white southern Democrats was nothing short of absolute upheaval. Mississippi had never been carried by a Republican candidate. In 1964, Goldwater won Mississippi with an astounding 87 percent of the vote.

Lyndon Johnson cruised to victory in one of the largest presidential landslides in history. Goldwater won only his home state and the Deep South, which had until that time been solidly and seemingly impenetrably Democratic. Republicans had finally broken the southern barrier. Those state presidential victories and the coinciding 1964 switch of former Dixiecrat candidate Strom Thurmond from the Democratic Party to the Republican Party would leave a lasting mark on both parties in the South.

The connection between the race issue and partisanship that was so obvious in 1964 would create opportunities and dilemmas for the Democrats and Republicans in the South. Democrats, of course, were pleased to welcome a loyal electoral base in the newly enfranchised African American community. Republicans were pleased to have broken the stranglehold of Democratic dominance in the South. However, Republicans, especially Republicans outside the South, did not want to be a party stigmatized by its 1964 presidential candidate's opposition to the Civil Rights and Voting Rights Acts. Democrats did not want to lose their otherwise loyal white base because of their party's strong stance on racial issues.

The Republican dilemma was faced directly and confronted forthrightly in Richard Nixon's 1968 campaign for the presidency when Nixon enlisted the help of Strom Thurmond's political advisers to devise a southern strategy that would appeal to Goldwater Democrats without resorting to the race issue. Although most Goldwater Democrats likely voted for Independent George Wallace in 1968 rather than Nixon, Republicans were persistent in wooing this constituency by using the Nixon strategy. Nixon showcased his tough stances on crime to southerners and contrasted his views with those of the "softer" Democrats. The issue appeared to work, and the strategy of appealing to white southerners through social issues that were not directly race related became more and more successful for Republicans in ensuing elections.

The Republican courtship of former Goldwater Democrats culminated in the enormously successful 1980 and 1984 appeals by Republican presidential candidate Ronald Reagan. He emphasized a variety of social and cultural issues and drew a line in the sand between the conservative Republican agenda and the more liberal Democratic agenda on everything from abortion to gun control to prayer in public schools. It worked, and the party system in the South was permanently altered. Republicans had found a place at the table in all of the South, including Louisiana. The social and cultural conservative message of the late twentieth century had supplanted the racial conservative message of 1964 and created loyal Republican voters in the once solidly Democratic South.

The ability of Republicans to win elections in the South had a snowball effect that spread beyond social and cultural issues. Once a two-party system was established, southerners who might have found the Republican Party attractive because of economic issues that had defined the party before Goldwater and Reagan, but who had always seen Republicans as hopelessly outgunned in the region, could now become active voters in a party that had a genuine chance to win elections. When the days of Democratic dominance ended, all kinds of Republicans, not just the newly converted, were able to participate fully. Republicans in the South quickly and firmly aligned themselves with interests to which nonsouthern Republicans were closely allied. The Republican Party in the South was now also the party of business and the party of small government. By the end of the twentieth century, the transformation from a Democrat-dominated South to a two-party South was complete.

. . . But Not Quite

The Republicans' conservative cultural and social message had catapulted them from the status of a nonplayer in southern party politics to that of the winning team in most national elections throughout the region. Remarkably, the full transformation took less than thirty years.

The two pivotal elements of the emergence of the two-party South are represented well in Louisiana politics, and in that sense Louisiana is very much a southern state. Blacks in Louisiana now form a steady base for

Democratic coalitions, and the cultural and social conservative message has become a fundamental, enduring part of the Republican appeal to many whites in the state. But unlike in Mississippi or Alabama, in Louisiana the result in elections for national offices is not always a win for the Republicans.

Since 1980, Republicans have won every presidential contest in Alabama and Mississippi. Republicans have won every race for the U.S. Senate in Mississippi since 1988. The last Democrat to win a Senate seat from Alabama was Richard Shelby in 1992, but he switched parties and became a Republican in 1994 and was easily reelected as a Republican in 1998.

By contrast, the Democrats have won two of the last six presidential elections in Louisiana (and in 1988 ran stronger in Louisiana than anywhere else in the South) and have won every Senate contest in the state. The point is not that Democrats dominate in Louisiana while Republicans dominate in Mississippi and Alabama. Rather, the point is that Democrats and Republicans are on a more equal footing in Louisiana than in the other two states.

Just as southern aspects of the Louisiana political culture explain the state's voting-pattern similarities to Mississippi and Alabama, the aspects of Louisiana culture not found in those states explain the differences. Like their Mississippi counterparts, Louisiana Democrats can count on a strong, consistent base among black voters and Louisiana Republicans can depend on a solid cultural conservative white base. Louisiana has both groups. In addition, however, it contains the French Catholic culture and the New Orleans culture, neither of which is found in Mississippi and Alabama.

Although Republicans have made dramatic gains in south Louisiana, the appeal of cultural conservatism is tempered in this French Catholic region. The 1964 southern breakthrough based on conservative Republican opposition to civil rights and voting rights was not as potent in south Louisiana as in the northern parishes. Indeed Catholic Acadian south Louisiana was the only part of the Deep South where blacks were voting in reasonable proportions before 1964. Since the deeply felt impulse toward states' rights stratagems to preserve segregation was not as strong in south Louisiana, the 1948 Dixiecrat revolt and the 1964 Republican southern breakthrough were not as meaningful there and thus did not root

Republican attitudes as firmly among whites in southern parishes as in northern Louisiana.

As the Republican Party moved quickly away from race to other cultural issues, more south Louisiana Catholics found the Republican platform appealing. Strong Republican opposition to abortion, and equally obvious national Democratic pro-choice positions, enticed south Louisiana Catholics in ways that the race issue did not. Indeed the emotional abortion issue proved to carry a valuable, potent political appeal for Republicans in several elections. In 1996, Republican U.S. Senate candidate Woody Jenkins gained ground in the last days of the election after a former Catholic archbishop publicly likened support for pro-choice Democratic candidate Mary Landrieu to religious blasphemy. Six days before the election, retired New Orleans archbishop Philip Hannan, speaking of Catholics voting for Landrieu despite her support for abortion rights, said, "If a person actually believes in Catholic doctrine, I don't see how they can avoid it being a sin."[16] The bombshell almost worked. Landrieu's relatively comfortable lead evaporated after the comment. Yet even though Catholics may be drawn to the Republican cultural conservative position on abortion, other stances, like the conservative position on gambling, are not as appealing, and white south Louisiana voters are still slightly less likely than their north Louisiana counterparts to vote Republican.

Not only were the European American (or white) cultures in Louisiana different, but in some significant ways the African American (or black) cultures are different as well. The existence of New Orleans has had the effect of making both the white and the black groups more urban on average than those in Mississippi and Alabama, and the preponderance of southern Europeans has the effect of making white voters slightly less conservative.

As early as the voting on secession from the Union in the 1860s, it was clear that New Orleans's citizens were unlike those in the rest of the South. In the 1860s the European American population in New Orleans was less committed to southern cultural values than citizens in the rest of the state and the rest of the South. That remains the case today. After the Civil War and in the century leading up to the Civil Rights Act and Voting Rights Act, the white voters in New Orleans were unlike the white voters in the rest of the South because many of them were not born in the South and did not share southern traditions and values. Even those whose families had lived in New Orleans for generations found themselves working and thriving in a more liberal social environment. The Republican appeal to "family values" issues that was so successful with whites in the South was particularly successful with white rural Protestants. Since white New Orleanians are mostly Catholic and by definition urban, these issues never produced the partisan upheaval in the city that they did elsewhere.

Black voters in New Orleans, like black voters throughout the South and the entire nation, are extremely loyal to the Democratic Party. Generalized support by African Americans in New Orleans has benefitted the Democratic Party in Louisiana even more than black votes have aided the party elsewhere in the South. The fact that a much larger proportion of African Americans live in an urban setting makes it easier for them to organize, participate, and avoid discrimination.

Compared with their rural counterparts, urban black voters naturally find it much easier to travel the smaller city distances to polling places, and the populous urban environment ensures public scrutiny of possible acts of racial discrimination by the news media or city officials. Turnout in rural areas is generally lower than in urban areas. Therefore, even though a larger proportion of the possible voting population in Mississippi is black, blacks almost always make up a larger proportion of the actual electorate in Louisiana.

The existence of New Orleans, in short, makes Democrats much more competitive in Louisiana than in the other states in the Deep South. In the closest United States Senate race in Louisiana history, in 1996 when Democrat Mary Landrieu defeated Republican Woody Jenkins by less than 6,000 votes, Landrieu carried New Orleans by around 100,000 votes. Whites in New Orleans were more likely to support the hometown Landrieu over the self-styled conservative Jenkins, while blacks in the city were well organized, found it easy to get to polling places, and turned out in very large numbers.

Had a race with similar candidates been held at the same time in Mississippi or Alabama, the Republican candidate would almost certainly have won easily. Jenkins's strong adherence to conservative issues clearly dampened support for him in New Orleans. His positions on these issues would not have been a problem in Mississippi where similar candidates, such as two-term governor Kirk Fordice, win frequently. Obviously the city of New Orleans has a dramatic effect on statewide party politics.

The 2000 Vote for President in Louisiana

The 2000 presidential exit poll (as reported by ABC News) is probably the most useful way to examine the breakdown in preferences of actual voters. Especially in the South, where the Republican Party is relatively new, many people still identify themselves as Democrats, even though they almost always vote Republican in elections for national offices like president, senator and member of Congress. The 2000 contest is also useful because it was a close election in which differences among groups for the two major party candidates can be clearly discerned.

Table 2-E (Appendix 2) shows the exit poll results for this election in Louisiana. The voter breakdown by race is stark. Self-identified blacks, who comprised 29 percent of this electorate, voted overwhelmingly for Democrat Gore. According to this survey, Gore received 92 percent of the black vote. Self-identified whites, who made up 70 percent of the group, voted 72 percent for Republican Bush and only 26 percent for Gore. While the split in preference by race is nothing short of staggering, it is consistent with historical patterns and historical events shaping party relationships with the races.

The Long-era-inspired economic pattern in voting is also quite evident in the 2000 election. Gore was the clear choice (more than 60 percent) among those with incomes less than $30,000 per year; Bush was an equally commanding choice for those with incomes above that amount.

The third major factor in voting patterns in the state—social or cultural issues—is a little more difficult to distinguish by group identification, but there are some reasonable, if not perfect, measures in the exit poll. Two questions appear to best identify voters as either social liberals or social conservatives.

The first, "Do you consider yourself part of the conservative Christian political movement known as the religious right?" In Louisiana, while the 22 percent of voters who answered "yes" to that question are very likely to be social conservatives, the 73 percent who answered "no" might include some socially conservative Catholics who do not consider themselves part of the religious right, which is normally associated with Protestant faiths. Nonetheless, this is a fairly useful distinction.

Among those who identified themselves as part of the religious right, 75 percent voted for Bush and 22 percent voted for Gore. Among the voters who did not identify themselves with the religious right, Gore won a 52 percent to 45 percent majority. This is certainly consistent with expectations that social conservatives are more likely to support Republicans.

The second question is, again, imperfect but useful: "On most political matters, do you consider yourself Liberal, Moderate, or Conservative?" The phrase "most political matters" could certainly include racial and economic issues as well as social issues, although identification of these terms with social issues is probably the most common connotation. Most respondents (43 percent) identified themselves as moderates, but 39 percent identified themselves as conservatives and 18 percent as liberals. Their voting preferences were, as expected, almost exactly reversed. Among liberals, Gore was the choice of 73 percent, and among conservatives Bush was the choice of 74 percent.

Clearly, the three factors in partisan vote choice, especially for elections to national offices, were at work in the 2000 presidential elections. African Americans, lower-income voters, and social liberals supported Gore. European Americans, higher-income voters, and social conservatives supported Bush.

If Louisiana's political culture is one of competition and instability, it should exhibit strong group identifications with political parties. Therefore, it is useful to compare Louisiana voting patterns with those of the rest of the nation. Sure enough, while these trends were also in effect in the nation as a whole (see table 2-F, Appendix 2), they were more pronounced in Louisiana.

The connection between race and vote choice, especially among whites, is stronger in Louisiana than in the nation as a whole. While blacks nationally were only slightly less likely to vote Democratic (90 percent compared to 92 percent), Louisiana whites were much more likely to vote Republican than whites nationwide (72 versus 54 percent). Thus the racial split is dramatic in Louisiana even when compared to the nation as a whole.

Partially because of the legacy of Longism, the correlation between income and voting is stronger in Louisiana as well. For example, while a very high 67 percent of the lowest-income respondents in Louisiana voted for Gore, nationally only 57 percent of the lowest-income category voted for Gore. Conversely, nationally only 54 percent of the highest-income voters were for Bush, while in Louisiana a whopping 73 percent of them preferred Bush. The pattern holds in every category (again, details are in table 5).

This pattern of Louisiana group identification having a stronger correlation to votes does not, however, hold with the groups identified by positions on social and cultural issues. For example, in Louisiana religious right preference for Bush, at 75 percent, was slightly less than the national average of 80 percent, and among those who identified themselves as conservative, 74 percent of Louisiana voters preferred the Republican, while 81 percent nationwide did the same. While this is likely at least in part due to the inadequacy of the questions, it may also be due to the lesser importance of these issues in Louisiana.

In order to shed some light on whether the weaker relationship between social issues and party in Louisiana is mostly due to the inadequacy of the questions or due to the weakness of social issues in determining votes in Louisiana, a comparison with a state where social issues are likely to be more important is worthwhile. In Mississippi, voters who identified themselves as members of the religious right preferred Bush at an astounding rate of 90 percent (as against 75 percent in Louisiana), and 82 percent of self-described conservatives (compared with 74 percent in Louisiana) voted Republican.

The three main political cleavages in Louisiana, defined by race, income, and social-cultural issues, were all at work in the 2000 presidential election. Connections between voter preference and groups defined by race and income was decidedly stronger in Louisiana than in the nation as a whole. There is somewhat weaker evidence (because of the inadequacy of survey questions) that the connections between vote preference and groups defined by positions on social and cultural issues is stronger outside Louisiana than in the state.

The 2002 United States Senate Election

While the 2000 presidential race provided a wealth of information about the Louisiana electorate, the 2002 election for the U.S. Senate provided enough drama to draw considerable national attention from the news media, fund raisers, and prominent politicians. A combination of factors thrust this contest into the national spotlight more than any Louisiana election since the 1991 runoff for governor between David Duke and Edwin Edwards. The election received intense, almost nonstop national attention in the weeks and days leading up to the runoff.

In 2002, incumbent Democrat Mary Landrieu was perceived as vulnerable because of her razor-thin margin of victory in 1996. In addition, Republican president George W. Bush was enjoying an almost unprecedented wave of popularity in the fall of 2002. Even so, as the election approached, Landrieu was expected to win because the Republican opposition had stumbled. But national political dynamics and Louisiana's odd election system combined to change the election from the expected yawner into a major political event.

Landrieu's most formidable opposition was supposed to be Monroe Republican congressman John Cooksey. His perceived strength appeared to keep many prominent Louisiana Republicans out of the race. A Landrieu vs. Cooksey head-to-head battle was not to be, however. The year before the election, as Cooksey was taking his first steps toward garnering statewide and national support for his run for the Senate, he made a comment on a statewide radio program that defined him and haunted his campaign throughout the next year. After the tragic events of September 11, 2001, Cooksey told reporter Jeff Palermo, "If I see someone come in and he's got a diaper on his head and a fan belt around that diaper on his head, that guy needs to be pulled over and checked."[17] The comment was reported widely and ran counter to the Bush administration's strongly expressed desire to keep religious and racial slurs out of the response to the attacks. Cooksey's campaign never seemed to recover. The negative reactions to the remark left Republicans outside the state unenthusiastic, and Cooksey began the race clearly handicapped.

Cooksey's problems left room for other Republican candidates to enter the race. The two most prominent were Baton Rouge state representative Tony Perkins, who had run Woody Jenkins's near-miss 1996 campaign against Landrieu, and Suzanne Haik Terrell, who had defeated Jenkins in a runoff for state commissioner of elections in 1999 to become the first female Republican to be elected to statewide office in Louisiana history. While Governor Mike Foster endorsed Cooksey, the National Republican Campaign Committee began funding the campaign of Terrell.

On November 5, 2002, national election day, Landrieu led the nine-person field with 46 percent of the vote. Terrell finished second with 27 percent and met Landrieu in a December 7 runoff. Louisiana's odd election system, which allowed for a runoff one month after all of the other United States Senate elections had been decided, shoved the battle into the spotlight. The national Republican Party, buoyed by victories across the country, turned its attention to Louisiana. Visits from President Bush, Vice President Cheney, and a laundry list of Republican political headliners, coupled with an infusion of money from both parties, made Louisiana the national electoral epicenter for the four-week runoff period.

Landrieu won the election by over 40,000 votes, a victory widely reported as a setback for President Bush and the Republicans and as a consolation to a national Democratic Party that had been badly bruised by the November elections. Landrieu won by energizing the two fundamental elements of Louisiana Democratic support, African American voters and economic issues. Terrell lost because she was not able to galvanize the Republican base of social and business conservatives. As map 2-A (Appendix 1) illustrates, Landrieu's strongest parishes were those with high proportions of African Americans, like Orleans and the Delta parishes in northeast Louisiana. She also received high vote proportions in the heavily unionized parishes between Baton Rouge and New Orleans. Terrell polled her best numbers in rural Protestant white north Louisiana parishes and the New Orleans suburbs.

Once again, racial, economic, and cultural cleavages explained much of the pattern of voting in a hotly contested two-party statewide race. This time, the Democrats won. While both parties have very well-defined constituencies, neither has a dependable majority. Therefore, two-party elections are likely to be highly competitive for the foreseeable future.

The 2003 Race for Governor

It would be difficult to imagine a governor's race that more clearly illustrates the state of constant change in Louisiana politics (and the thesis of this book) than the 2003 election. In the fall of that year, seven major candidates ran to succeed two-term incumbent Republican governor Mike Foster, who was barred by the state constitution from running for a third consecutive term. For those who love to watch the unconventional colorful politics of Louisiana, this governor's race, although tame by the standards set by the Longs and Edwin Edwards, did not disappoint.

The contrast to the notorious 1991 governor's election was striking. Only twelve years earlier, Louisiana had witnessed a runoff for governor between two candidates who represented the politics of the past. Edwin Edwards was a Long-style populist, and David Duke was best known for his association with the Ku Klux Klan. By contrast, in 2003, the runoff for governor was between two candidates who represented something very new. They were widely hailed as "firsts" for Louisiana. Republican Piyush "Bobby" Jindal, the thirty-two-year-old Ivy League–educated "policy wonk" who had never held elective office, would be the nation's first Indian American governor. Democrat Kathleen Babineaux Blanco, a two-term lieutenant governor and former state legislator and state public service commissioner, would be Louisiana's first woman governor. In Louisiana, where volatility in institutions and electoral behavior is the norm, the contrast between the Duke-Edwards and Blanco-Jindal races was another indication that change itself is politics-as-usual.

In the early summer of 2003, at least ten potential candidates appeared to have some chance of making the runoff in a wide-open race. By the August filing date, the field had narrowed to seven major contenders—four Democrats and three Republicans. Around 20 percent of the vote seemed to be a logical target to secure a place in the November 15 runoff, and each of the candidates had obvious strategies to attain this goal. The top two candidates, regardless of party, would make the runoff unless—as seemed highly unlikely—one candidate gained over 50 percent of the vote in the first election. In general the Democrats were better known and, at the outset, better funded than the Republican candidates.

Of the four Democrats, state attorney general Richard Ieyoub, who had barely missed a runoff spot in the 1996 election for the U.S. Senate, was as close to a consensus favorite as any candidate in the race. His strategy was to secure the Democratic base. He was very well known and worked hard to gain endorsements from the African American community, from labor groups, and from teachers and law enforcement groups. His plan may well have been foolproof had it not been for the existence of another candidate who had a similar strategy.

Former state representative and congressman Claude "Buddy" Leach targeted almost exactly the same voters as Ieyoub. Although not nearly as well known as Ieyoub, not having run for office in over a decade, he was considered a formidable candidate because his personal wealth could allow him to overcome lower name-recognition. His television commercials were running a year before the election, competing with the advertisements in the hotly contested U.S. Senate race—and he become an almost instant threat to Ieyoub's campaign.

With no major African American candidate in the race, and since

African Americans make up around 25 percent of the typical electorate in Louisiana, both Ieyoub and Leach had a real chance to be in the runoff if they could secure most of those votes and add to them other parts of the Democratic base. Both candidates spent millions of dollars and campaigned hard until the day before the runoff, but neither faded enough to allow the other to garner a large enough coalition to run higher than third (Ieyoub) and fourth (Leach).

The Ieyoub and Leach focus on traditional Democratic voters forced the other two Democrats to adopt more centrist strategies, hoping to build a coalition of Democrats and some Republicans. Lieutenant Governor Kathleen Blanco had won her last race with 86 percent of the vote and was polling at the top of almost all of the voter surveys during the spring, summer, and early fall of 2003. Despite those quite formidable accomplishments, her candidacy was often discounted in the media by her opponents as simply a testament to her name recognition. She was also haunted by the history of dismal failure of past lieutenant governors in their quest for the top office. Her chances were logically compared with those of her predecessor, Melinda Schwegmann, who eight years earlier had begun her campaign for governor with a big lead in the polls, only to see it fade fast and end the race toward the back of the pack.

Blanco, however, had a political advantage that Schwegmann was missing. While Schwegmann was competing for votes in her home base of New Orleans with fellow Democrat Mary Landrieu, Kathleen *Babineaux* (emphasis added) Blanco was the lone candidate from the important swing-vote area of Lafayette and surrounding parishes. A pro-life Democrat in Catholic Acadiana can run well even among Republicans, and Blanco was perfectly positioned to get those votes. In addition, as a Democrat who was well known statewide, she could pick up Democratic votes elsewhere as well. And even though she did, indeed, start slipping in the polls as the election approached, it was a strategy that worked well enough to place second and make it to the runoff.

Finally, Democrat Randy Ewing, a former president of the state senate, had a strategy similar to Blanco's. He ran a nonideological campaign, emphasizing his record as a legislator and businessman, and hoped to build on his home base in north Louisiana, where, like Blanco in the Lafayette area, he was the sole candidate. Unlike Blanco, however, he needed money and time to build statewide name recognition, and despite some impressive endorsements, like that of first-term New Orleans mayor Ray Nagin, Ewing ran last among the major Democrats and placed fifth overall in the October 4 election.

While all four Democratic candidates were fighting for votes up until the day of the October election, the Republicans separated themselves into "front runner" and "long shot" a few weeks before election day. The biggest story was Jindal.

Suburban pro-business middle- and upper-income voters are a key part of Republican support, especially the financial base, in Louisiana, but rural social conservatives provide the biggest share of the Republican vote. Eight years earlier Mike Foster had taken his campaign from a blip in the voter surveys to the governorship with the often-repeated message, "I'm a Christian and a gun owner." It was a point not lost on the three major Republican candidates, and the candidate who on the surface appeared to have the least chance with these voters, Bobby Jindal, ran a brilliant campaign targeted to these voters and emerged on top in the October election.

In midsummer, the incumbent Foster announced that he was supporting Jindal, whom he had appointed to major state bureaucratic positions and who had served nationally as a Health and Human Services official in the George W. Bush administration. The governor's announcement received a mixed response. Although Jindal was widely perceived as being a star of the Foster administration, his youth, his lack of any elective political experience, and—the biggest curiosity—his Indian American heritage all brought into question his ability to run successfully for governor. Those concerns lost their edge when Jindal quickly raised large sums of money for his campaign and began a meteoric rise in the voter surveys. His campaign strategy was extremely effective. While he may have had some natural appeal to suburban business voters because of his policy experience and his Ivy League education, he centered his media campaign on ads on conservative talk radio throughout the state, aiming specifically at those voters who had helped elect Foster four years earlier. The ads emphasized his Christian values and criticized "liberal" judges and other politicians. The radio campaign was spectacularly successful, and Jindal's rise in the polls reflected his strong momentum in the last weeks before the October 4 election, in which he finished a strong first with 32 percent of the vote, a full 14 points above second-place finisher Kathleen Blanco.

The two other major Republican candidates each appeared to have a strong appeal to social conservatives. Public Service Commissioner Jay Blossman, who had briefly run for the United States Senate a year earlier, ran a series of advertisements that focused attention squarely on messages that had appealed to social conservatives in the past. Blossman's ads featured criticism of the pet projects of high-profile African American state senator Cleo Fields and bluntly criticized the state legislature for preferring spending money on those programs to providing more funding for the investigation of the Baton Rouge serial killer. The Blossman campaign ads were provocative and the subject of countless news stories and conversations on talk radio. The Blossman campaign included a highly publicized teaming with conservative former congressman Clyde Holloway, who was running for lieutenant governor. While the campaign was widely discussed and seemed to be well targeted, Blossman's poll numbers never rose above the low single digits, and in the last week of the campaign he withdrew to support the third major Republican candidate, former Speaker of the Louisiana House of Representatives Hunt Downer.

Ironically, Downer's candidacy never recovered from the strong endorsement he received from several prominent Republican fund-raisers and politicians in late summer. Concerned that too many Republicans were considering running for governor, these supporters had held an all-too-publicized "closed door" meeting to winnow down the field. Downer had emerged the winner, and two other candidates—John Hainkel, the president of the state senate, and Dave Treen, a former governor—dropped out and supported him. The public must have seen this negatively, because despite high expectations and the endorsement of popular Republican congressman Billy Tauzin, the Downer campaign never gained much momentum and, with Blossman out, Downer finished last among the major candidates in the first election. Downer's troubles may have been less a result of the failure of his own strategy and more a result of the extraordinary success of the Jindal campaign in capturing Downer's targeted voters.

With Democrats Ieyoub, Leach, and Ewing and Republicans Downer and Blossman aside, Louisiana awoke on October 5 to a runoff for governor between two candidates that many had not seen as likely final contenders, and almost assuredly most would not have picked to be the sole two standing.

In the end, it was Blanco who made history. She was able to mobilize the Democratic coalition and combine that with her Lafayette area base to become the first woman elected governor in Louisiana history.

Kathleen Blanco and Bobby Jindal were at once a sign of change and of continuity. As a woman and an Indian American, they were unlike any governor's runoff in Louisiana history. But they were also examples of the constancy of Louisiana's highly volatile political culture.

Elections in a Disorderly Democracy

Although Louisianians do not vote in greater percentages than any other state citizens, Louisiana does spend an inordinate amount of time, skill, and money on elections. In a state where politics is so unstable and disorderly, it is not surprising that elections are held for almost every conceivable post and that unusually large amounts of money are spent to win those elections.

The election rules themselves can turn this game into an anything-goes competition. No one outside the state understands them very well because they break all of the norms about party primaries and general elections. People inside the state understand, probably intuitively, that the rules are there because they helped some politicians consolidate their power—and that the next time a strong coalition of winners sees an opportunity to change the rules to benefit them, the election laws might well change again.

The most telling ramification of the Louisiana political culture on elections is the effect on voting patterns. While Louisiana voting patterns may be confusing to the outsider, to those familiar with Louisiana culture, the patterns are not confusing at all if they are understood as a reflection of the Louisiana political culture. In fact, Louisiana electoral politics may be one of a kind when compared to electoral politics in other states, but they are easy to understand when compared to all of the other characteristics of politics within the state. North Louisiana is mostly rural and Protestant, and whites there often vote Republican, much like rural white Protestants in most of the rest of the South. In French Catholic south Louisiana the new Republican conservative social message is a mixed bag, and therefore the voting patterns are mixed as well. African Americans in Louisiana are loyal to the Democratic Party, like blacks all over the country, because of the party's visible, well-nurtured relationship with the black community.

New Orleans is home not only to a large urban black population but to numerous white voters whose roots are not as firmly connected to conservative cultural issues as those of their rural and suburban counterparts; therefore, New Orleans is a major building block of any Democratic victory.

Another reason Louisiana voting patterns sometimes come closer to national voting patterns than to southern voting patterns is the significance of economic class voting. Fifty years of Long and anti-Long election rhetoric of pocketbook issues, share-the-wealth programs, and haves versus have-nots accustomed Louisianians to voting along economic class lines. Even the 2000 election for president showed this pattern. Economic pattern voting may also simply be the alternative to cultural pattern voting: when cultural issues are weaker, voters identify more with their economic status.

Louisiana's three well-defined ethnic groups do not translate into three well-defined voting coalitions. The coexistence of the three produces unique participation patterns and voting patterns. When played out on the field of an unusual election system, these cultural twists and historical circumstances have, perhaps inevitably, made Louisiana politics an even more competitive sport.

3. Government

The Most Powerful?

It is a little disconcerting to grow up in Louisiana hearing your grandparents and parents and all of the local news media mentioning as a matter of fact that Louisiana has THE MOST POWERFUL GOVERNOR IN THE UNITED STATES! and then pick up a textbook on state government and find Louisiana unceremoniously listed somewhere near the middle of the pack in terms of gubernatorial power (see tables 3-A and 3-B, Appendix 2).

The executive branch is not the only part of Louisiana's government that is the subject of superlatives and hyperbole. The stories of the hijinks and shenanigans of the legislature are probably at least on a par with those of any other state. Louisiana's judicial system also is mentioned with a dramatic flair and pride that seem odd for discussions of a branch of government that normally stands in the shadows of the other two. Louisianians are quick to blame or credit the infamous, and almost universally misunderstood, Napoleonic Code for the idiosyncrasies of their legal system.

All three—the governor, the legislature, and the courts—deserve a systematic analysis of whether they are indeed unique and how they reflect the Louisiana political culture.

The Emperor May Have No Clothes, but He Wears Them Well

Louisiana governors are legendary. Huey Long, Earl Long, and Edwin Edwards were immensely powerful occupants of the office. Can all of those grandparents be that wrong? In Ken Burns's award-winning documentary on Huey Long, the narrator reminds the viewer more than once that Huey Long had amassed more power in Louisiana than any one person had in the history of the United States. How, then, can social scientists dare to put Louisiana in the middle of the list?

The legend is fundamentally true, but the legend and the indexes of gubernatorial power are addressing two different things—the power of the office and the power exerted by the inhabitants of the office, the governors themselves. The powers of the office of governor in Louisiana, especially since the passage of the present state constitution in 1974, are unremarkable. But the power exerted by holders of the office has been nothing short of spectacular—all the more so given the limited actual powers that the office confers on these men who want to be king.

It is difficult to measure the actual power exerted by a governor over a state, but a wealth of evidence suggests that well beyond the reign of Huey Long, Louisiana governors have exerted extraordinary influence in state policy-making. Until 1991, when the legislature overturned Governor Charles "Buddy" Roemer's veto of an abortion bill, no Louisiana governor's veto had been overridden in recorded history—or at least not since the inception of the previous Constitution in 1921. Roemer regularly tells the Louisiana Government class at LSU about his first days in office sitting at (metaphorically) the same desk where Huey and Earl sat and beginning to sense that, indeed, he had an enormous amount of power. Roemer describes the reaction he received from legislators once he was elected: a reaction of strong deference. He must be powerful because he is the governor of Louisiana—and "we all know" that the Louisiana governor is THE MOST POWERFUL GOVERNOR IN THE UNITED STATES!

Especially since the institution of the present constitution, the power of the office of the governor of Louisiana in most of the areas normally measured is unspectacular at best. As any textbook will report, the Louisiana governor has all of the normal budgetary powers such as line-item veto, but because of the tradition of electing practically everything, Louisiana's chief executive actually has less than normal appointment powers. In the compilation of gubernatorial powers most widely cited among academics, Thad Beyle lists Louisiana at number thirty-seven, well below the heavy hitters—New Jersey, Pennsylvania, Utah, Hawaii, and Maryland (see table 3-A). Why, then, do most Louisianians assume otherwise?

Perhaps it is context. Geographically, Louisiana is between Texas (number forty-five) and Mississippi (number forty-four), states with notoriously weak governors, and it may therefore appear to have a strong chief executive simply by comparison. Probably not. The answer more likely lies in the shrewd political instincts of the three dominant figures in Louisiana politics in the twentieth century. They are easily identified by their first names—Huey, Earl, and Edwin.

Huey's Desk

If Louisiana governors have indeed wielded disproportionate power, at least part of the reason is the legacy of Huey Long. The four years that Huey served as governor set a pattern for the relationship between the governor and the legislature that endured for most of the remainder of the twentieth century. Long's power rested in his populist politics. Like all populists of the day, he campaigned and won as a leader of the common people against the entrenched business and government interests. He emerged in a time when southerners were rapidly expanding the right to participate in politics to poorer whites—women and African American voting movements would come later. These poorer, less educated, mostly rural white men were the force that drove and supported populist politicians throughout the South (and the rest of the nation) around the turn of the twentieth century.

Two Pulitzer Prize–winning books by former LSU professors have helped to give Huey Long a reputation as perhaps the most masterful populist of the bunch. T. Harry Williams's biography *Huey Long* and Robert Penn Warren's *All the King's Men,* a novel widely interpreted as a thinly disguised depiction of Long's career, made the nation and the world aware of how skillfully and ruthlessly Long seized on a newly opened opportunity.[1] Huey knew that thousands and thousands of poor rural whites who were finally securing the right to vote could, by virtue of their sheer numbers, enable a smart politician to become a mighty force. In *All the King's Men,* Warren was obviously concerned about the possibility of this new majority exercising power Warren did not think it was ready to exercise.

Long harnessed the fierce personal loyalty of these heretofore ignored masses in Louisiana. He began his political career by easily winning a seat on the state Railroad Commission (the forerunner to the Public Service Commission), where he could create a very public persona as a champion of the common man against the political and business bigwigs who had been running the state. He gained a reputation as the politician who not only would fight for the common man but could often actually win—for instance, by beating back rises in utility rates. His appeal as a potent populist became the lifeblood of his enormous political strength.

In 1924, at the young age of thirty-one, Huey ran for governor. From his base in the north Louisiana Railroad Commission District, he ran a skillful campaign and placed a very respectable third in the Democratic primary. That showing made him a credible statewide politician and a force to be confronted. He ran again in 1928 and won. The "common man" message had worked, and Long stormed into office with a clear populist agenda. In the four short years he served as governor, he used the prerogatives of the office in ways never before seen.

The stories are legendary. Huey threatened to use an obscure state animal-dipping law to prod the Barnum and Bailey Circus into moving the date of their show so it would not conflict with an LSU football game. When legislators refused to allocate money to build a new, showy governor's mansion that would befit a man of his stature, he ordered state penitentiary inmates to demolish the old one—and then was given the funds for the new structure. He pushed funding for the present towering state capitol—still the tallest in the nation at 450 feet—by working the back of the legislative chambers when the bill was a few votes short of passage. Almost everything he built was bigger, fancier, and much more expensive than it needed to be.

The thread that runs through these stories is the way Huey used mass support in order to increase his control of the state. He would do outlandish things that were wildly popular among his core constituency and then dare the legislature or the courts to defy him. Public support became a stockpile of ammunition with which to fight for what he wanted against established politicians and big businesses, especially the oil and gas companies.

Huey Long was also a masterful campaigner. T. Harry Williams begins his biography of Long with a story that even Williams admits "seems too good to be true."[2] He tells of Long crisscrossing the state and at every stop recounting how he picked up his grandmother every Sunday morning and drove her in their horse and buggy to church. In north Louisiana, Long would always say that he drove her to a Baptist church; in south Louisiana, the grandmother worshiped in a Catholic church. When asked about which account was correct, Long answered, "Don't be a damn fool. We didn't even have a horse!"[3] The truth about whether he was Baptist or Catholic—or whether indeed he went to church or could afford a car—was immaterial to Long. What mattered was that he identified with the masses and they identified right back.

It worked. Huey turned the current political establishment on its head and seemed to scare its members to death. Alan Brinkley characterized the monumental impact of the success of Long's populist strategy in winning the 1928 race for governor:

> The 1928 election revealed a pattern new to Louisiana politics, a pattern startling and disturbing to those members of the old guard who could perceive what happened. Political divisions in the state had traditionally followed ethnic and religious lines: Protestant against Catholic, Anglo-Saxon against Creole, north against south. Suddenly everything had changed. Huey Long, who had lost the election four years earlier at least in part because of cultural and religious issues brought to the fore by the Ku Klux Klan, had now assembled a majority coalition that reflected the sharp economic divisions in the state.[4]

And, as Brinkley notes, Long and his followers knew what had happened:

> It was little wonder, then, that the lobby of the Roosevelt Hotel in New Orleans, Long's campaign headquarters, was a scene of pandemonium and exultation on election night. Crowds jammed every corner; campaign workers slapped one another on the back, whooping in triumph. And slowly the crush moved Huey Long, shirt open at the neck, hair tousled, eyes bloodshot, face red. As he reached for the eager hands pressing at him from all sides, his tired, hoarse voice expressed his confidence in the future: "We'll show 'em who's boss . . . You fellers stick by me . . . We're just getting started."[5]

From that day onward the Long message, personified in the near-caricature of himself that Long created, was heard in every statewide campaign in Louisiana for almost fifty years.

This method of pumping up his strength through populist appeals rose to a higher level midway through Long's term. The event that had the most enduring and dramatic impact on the office of governor actually arose from a Long defeat. In 1929, after he tried unsuccessfully to pass a tax on petroleum, Long was charged with nineteen counts of impeachment. The tax had been the last straw to a legislature that had tired of Long's almost tyrannical power plays. The state house of representatives approved eight of the nineteen counts of impeachment. Long's governorship could now be terminated by the will of two-thirds of the Louisiana senate. Long was infuriated. Before matters could deteriorate further, he secured signed promises from enough senators to ensure his acquittal. The trial never took place.

From that moment on, Long no longer found it necessary to pay even lip service to the niceties of the governmental process. He made it abundantly clear to anyone who would listen that in his eyes the impeachment was obvious evidence that the government of Louisiana was controlled by the big-oil, big-money interests and the only hope for the common people was to fight fire with fire. Long became the loud voice of the masses in a struggle against the elites, and he was applauded by his supporters when he was able to show them that he was boss. He was intoxicated by the energy that they gave him and, from the impeachment onward, amassed so much power that his enemies would prophetically talk of the inevitability of Long's assassination as the only way to stop him.

By the end of his term, Long was widely viewed as having more control over the state than any politician had held in the history of the United States. Long had used his popular support to expand the power of the governorship to unheard-of levels. Masterful politicians in other states in the South were not as successful as Long in building an enduring coalition of poor whites and, therefore, did not have as lasting an impact on the office itself. Long split the Democratic Party of Louisiana into two well-defined coalitions of "haves" (anti-Longs) and "have-nots" (Longs) that endured beyond his death and well into the second half of the century. This Long era of bifactionalism, or two factions within one dominant party, has fascinated journalists, historians, and political scientists for decades. "Longism" was more than a name for poor people's politics and policy. "Longism" also came to symbolize dominance of the political system by one person.

Long's raw intelligence and political skills were certainly extraordinary. But his setting—Louisiana—contributed to his success as well. Long was able to produce such fierce devotion in his followers because he not only made spectacular, unprecedented promises to the voters but was able to deliver on them. The vast natural oil and gas resources in Louisiana allowed Long to tax this new and prosperous major industry and fund all of the programs that poor people wanted—and often much more than they wanted.

Texas, Oklahoma, and Alaska all reaped their own stupendous financial windfalls from oil and gas. But it was Louisiana where the impact was greatest. Texas could secure more oil-and-gas-related taxes, but Texas had five or six times the population of Louisiana. When oil-and-gas-related revenue is considered as a proportion of a state budget, no other state can compare with Louisiana. While officials in neighboring Texas eventually dedicated most of its rich petrochemical revenues to a specified fund for higher education, Huey Long in Louisiana did not. He used the money on visible structures and on people and programs that, in turn, made still more people indebted to him. The natural resources in Louisiana provided the money for this brilliant man to secure unprecedented loyalty and power.

Another feature of the Louisiana culture, not available in other states, allowed Long to practice his politics of helping the poor by taxing the rich. In other southern states where the populist message provided a strong base of support among newly empowered poor whites, racism became the central rallying cry because it was a message that resonated well and that did not cost much money.

One notorious example of this phenomenon was Tom Watson of Georgia, who began his populist career with the admirable intention of uniting economically deprived Georgians of all races but changed, like so many others after him (George Wallace of Alabama being perhaps the most familiar in relatively recent history), into a bombastic, inflammatory racist in order to secure the devotion of the legions of poor white voters. Huey Long was a rare exception in the use of racial rhetoric among southern populist politicians. Although he did not promote racial equality or integration, he pointedly did not fan the fires of racism in his speeches.

Huey's brother and fellow governor Earl Long was pointed in his comments about race. In fact, he was fighting to end the purging of black voters when he became so enraged in front of the legislature that he was taken to a mental hospital. A. J. Liebling, in *The Earl of Louisiana,* quotes a campaign speech in which Earl, before an outdoor audience of both races, was addressing the latest plans of powerful and outspoken segregationist state senator Willie Rainach:

> "That's the way I like to see it," the Governor said, from the stand. "Not all our colored friends in one spot and white friends in another. I'm the best friend the poor white man, and the middle-class white man, and the rich white man—so long as he behaves himself—and the poor colored man, ever had in the State of Loosiana. And if the NAACP and the little pea-headed nut Willie Rainach will just leave

us alone, then *sen*sible people, not cranks, can get along in a *rea*sonable way. That Rainach wants to fight the Civil War all over again."[6]

The Long brothers' relatively enlightened stance on racial matters was partially due to their family background. They were products of a significant southern white tradition of opposition to black oppression. Their grandfather had opposed secession from the Union. This heritage, coupled with the history of racial moderation in the French Catholic southern part of the state, required Huey Long to find other ways to appeal to his "common man." Huey's (and Earl's) populist rhetoric was by necessity more economic than racial: diatribes against the rich and powerful were essential to his message; race hatred was not. This rhetoric was more enduring, easier to act upon (blacks were already oppressed), and more exportable outside of Louisiana than pure racial demagoguery. Huey's nonracist populism allowed him to use his considerable skills to become a national political force, which only served to heighten his stature and fame inside the state.

The Long Legacy

The precedent that Huey Long set in his single term as governor lasted for several decades. Two of his successors, his brother Earl and four-term governor Edwin Edwards, cemented the pattern that Huey started of dominant personalities manipulating the powers of the office. In some ways, Earl flashed even more bravado than Huey. A. J. Liebling describes one of the more infamous examples in the following description of Earl Long trying to skirt the constitutional limitation at that time of one-term governorships: "Earl, in entering the primaries, was challenging the Louisiana constitution, which provides that a governor may not succeed himself directly. Earl, bowing to this law, had dropped out after his 1948–52 term and then had returned in 1956. Now, however, he was raising the point that if he resigned before election—the formal, post-primary, election, that is—his Lieutenant Governor would become Governor, and so he, coming in to begin a new term, would be succeeding not himself but the fellow who had succeeded him. Even Huey had not thought of that one."[7]

Earl's scheme ultimately failed, but it was a genuine indication of how he approached the office. Earl was more successful in using his infamous machinations to free himself from a state mental hospital and return to the governor's chair in 1959. Michael Kurtz and Morgan Peoples lay out the details of this outlandish saga in their biography *Earl K. Long: The Saga of Uncle Earl and Louisiana Politics:*

> During an address before a joint legislative session, Long had spoken incoherently and irrationally, personally denouncing his political opponents and launching into outbursts of obscenities. After speaking extemporaneously for an hour and a half, Long could not continue and had to be escorted from the podium. Taken to the Governor's Mansion, he was confined to an upstairs bedroom, with two burly hospital attendants as guards. After consulting with family members and with physicians, Long's estranged wife, Blanche, sister Lucille, and his nephew, Russell, decided to have him committed to a mental institution. The following morning, Long was flown in a Louisiana National Guard airplane to Galveston, Texas, where he was admitted to the Titus Harris Psychiatric Clinic of John Sealy Hospital, a respected facility that had agreed to admit him. After spending over two weeks at the Galveston facility, Earl secured his release by filing a habeas corpus lawsuit against Blanche and by promising to undergo treatment at the Ochsner Foundation Hospital near New Orleans. The governor did indeed go to Ochsner's, but he stayed only a few hours and departed for Baton Rouge. Upon learning of his action, Blanche notified the East Baton Parish coroner to draw up the legal papers necessary to have her husband committed to a state mental institution. When Earl reached the East Baton Rouge Parish line, he was met by sheriff's deputies, who transported him to the parish courthouse. After a perfunctory psychiatric examination, he was forcibly and involuntarily taken to Mandeville in St. Tammany Parish, where he was committed to the Southeast Louisiana Hospital. Earl remained in Mandeville for nine days, during which time he had his attorney, Joe Arthur Sims, file a separation suit against Blanche, thereby legally preventing her from recommitting him. Earl then fired the head of the state Hospital Board, Jesse H. Bankston, and replaced him with a friend, Charles Rosenblum. Rosenblum persuaded the board to fire the acting superintendent at Mandeville, Dr. Charles H. Belcher, and hire Dr. Jess H. McClendon. A close friend of Earl's, Dr. McClendon immediately ordered him re-

> leased from Mandeville. In a highly publicized court hearing in nearby Covington, Judge Robert Jones ruled that Governor Long could no longer be legally confined in the institution and was therefore a free man.[8]

Earl Long certainly governed in Huey's style. Earl could appear foolish and yet keep the loyalty of his constituents because he delivered on his promises to his supporters. Earl, like Huey, portrayed himself as a governor on the side of poor people who needed services, and he used the vast oil-and-gas-related resources of the state in order to provide basic needs for an underclass that felt it was ignored by other politicians. This ability to personify the supply of goods and services to the poor served to strengthen the governorship enormously and provided a model for the state's third powerhouse governor of the twentieth century, Edwin W. Edwards.

No-Tell Motel Window

Although the 1960s are correctly perceived as the end of the Long era, the circumstances that enabled and empowered kingpin governors certainly did not end with that era. Edwin Edwards astutely realized that the tumultuous sixties may have revolutionized many things about Louisiana politics, but they did not revolutionize the opportunities for gubernatorial domination.

Long-era bifactionalism withered in the 1960s for three main reasons. The first was fittingly melodramatic. Earl Long did not follow through on his scheme to run for a second consecutive term in 1959 but instead ran for lieutenant governor in an attempt to hold onto his powers. It failed when he finished third in the Democratic primary and missed the runoff. In 1960 he tried to revive his bruised ego and ran against incumbent Harold McSween for a seat in Congress from Louisiana's sprawling Eighth Congressional District, anchored in Alexandria. The runoff between Long and the incumbent was vintage Earl. Michael Kurtz and Morgan Peoples chronicle the tragic, truth-is-stranger-than-fiction events of the last days of the election:

> On Friday, August 26, 1960, Earl Long celebrated his sixty-fifth birthday, and his cousin Ed Wingate advised him to take the day off, relax, and have a good time. But Earl refused. It was the day before the

second primary, and he still had last-minute politicking to conduct. He told Wingate, "Ed, I've got a long time to rest. If I could beat him, I'd die happy." So he stumped the two pivotal parishes in the district, Rapides and Avoyelles, visiting country stores and calling on local farmers. Thus, Earl ended his political career the way he began it forty years earlier, hustling votes from the poor black and white farmers in rural Louisiana. The following day, Saturday, August 27, was the election, and as he awaited the returns in a room at the Bentley Hotel in Alexandria, Earl Long suffered a severe heart attack. Refusing his family's pleas to go to the hospital, he told reporters that he felt a little "puny" from eating "overripe pork," and he spent the day, as he did during every election, on the telephone, contacting key people to ensure that they got out the vote. Only after the polls closed at 8:00 P.M. did he allow his family to have him taken to the hospital. In the election, Earl pulled off what many considered the most spectacular upset of his career by defeating McSween, 38,693 votes to 34,235. His incessant campaigning in the rural areas resulted in a huge country turnout, easily offsetting McSween's expected heavy vote in Alexandria and Marksville. By the thousands, poor black and white farmers, many of whom had never voted before, showed up at the polls to cast their ballots for their beloved Uncle Earl. One dedicated black supporter in Colfax proudly boasted that "I've been up 'til three o'clock every morning the past two weeks working for Uncle Earl. I have got him sixty votes, I bet." The country folk who gave him his last political victory did so out of appreciation for all the things he had done for them over the years, for they knew this would be his last campaign.[9]

Earl died ten days later. This melodramatic ending to the Long era in Louisiana only masked the deeper causes for its demise. Two fundamental factors that had profoundly changed the Louisiana political landscape had led to Earl's statewide defeat and the lack of any clearly Long/anti-Long battles in the future. The first was the emerging civil rights movement. The Longs were able to ignore racial conflict when blacks did not pose an immediate threat to the jobs, housing, and access to public accommodations of poorer whites, but when demands for these things gained ground, Longites could no longer promise simply to help poor whites. They must also address the growing, visible needs and desires of blacks in Louisiana, which were increasingly at odds with the attitudes of Earl Long's poorer white constituents.

A. J. Liebling analyzes what he sees as the fatal impact of the race issue on Long-era bifactionalism:

> This issue turned out to be Earl Long's tragedy. His views on race were much like those of Huey. He thought it an artificial question in politics. The real problems were economic in nature, and a leader's concern should be how to attain the power to deal with them. But at the same time he, and also Huey, realized that Negroes were poor people, the poorest of the poor, and had to be included in any programs of social uplift. It was an awareness that set the Longs apart from virtually all Southern popular leaders, who saw the blacks only as a vague group on the fringes of white society or as a menace to be conjured up at election time.[10]

The Longite practice of building support and gubernatorial power by taxing the petrochemical industry and providing social, educational, and health services for the poor was being overshadowed by national government's insistence that African American rights be granted. The Long/anti-Long rhetoric did not adapt well to the emerging politically destructive divide between poor whites and blacks, and Earl's appeal waned.

In his description of Earl Long's final days, A. J. Liebling also touched on the reason for the final demise of Longism itself when he noted that Earl "ended his career the way he began it forty years earlier, hustling votes from poor black and white farmers in rural Louisiana."[11] Longism depended on door-to-door, face-to-face connections with people. It was the feel, the touch, the handshake that made the Longs' followers believers in themselves and in the Longs. By 1960, the rise of television politics began to take that away. On television, Huey and Earl would more likely have been perceived as country bumpkins than "one of us." In the lingo of the classic Marshall McLuhan work *Understanding Media*, the Longs were suited to the "warm" politics of stump speeches and radio addresses.[12] Television had brought to Louisiana the "cool" politics of smooth delivery and clean visual lines.

The changing factor of race politics and the new factor of television did not deter Edwin Edwards from continuing the legacy of gubernatorial supremacy. He adapted to them. He used his Cajun background to build an ethnic bridge over the race issue and appeal to both the French ethnic working class and blacks. It was brilliant and it worked. He reveled in being an ethnic minority, speaking Cajun French loudly and proudly in Acadiana during his campaigns. Working-class Cajuns had become accustomed to the civil rights movement's successes and were not going to vote against the man who could be the first Cajun governor of Louisiana simply because he was also the choice of black voters.

Edwards and Made-for-TV Longism

Edwards seemed born for television. His persona was "cool" in stark contrast to the "warm" personalities of the Long brothers. If television would not have been kind to Huey or Earl Long, Edwards's hair, his suits, his speaking style, his understated wit were all, whether planned or not, perfect for television.

Edwin Edwards was born on August 7, 1927, in a rural area near Marksville, Louisiana, in Avoyelles Parish, the northernmost of the French Catholic parishes. He graduated from LSU Law School at twenty-one and began practicing law in Crowley, Louisiana, the place most associated with him as his home. He was elected to the Crowley city council in 1954, to the Louisiana state senate, and three times to Congress from the Seventh Congressional District, which covers most of southwest Louisiana. In 1971, he made his first run for governor.

Edwards was elected governor an unprecedented four times, and he defined and dominated Louisiana politics of the last third of the twentieth century. Edwards was a television, post–Civil Rights Act populist, and he continued the traditions of gubernatorial prowess that made his role models Huey and Earl Long famous and infamous. Edwards's understanding of the populist basis of gubernatorial strength is best demonstrated in his support for some major institutional changes that would seem self-defeating for any governor who wants to control a state's politics. Edwards did not care. He presided over sweeping reforms that gave the legislature much greater power in its relationship with the office of governor. Edwards was so confident in his ability to control politics that he was happy to give the "good government" groups a victory in constitutional reform. He seemed to know that a governor's power in Louisiana had less to do with power derived from rules and procedures and much more to do with power derived from mass support.

Edwards's rise and slow denouement traced some fundamental changes in the state economic environment. He was elected in 1971 and reelected in a landslide in 1975 when the state was experiencing an economic boom thanks to oil and gas revenues. He was the "Good Times" governor and he seemed to represent so much that was positive about Louisiana. Like Huey and Earl Long before him, Edwin Edwards made common Louisianians feel great about themselves. And like Huey and Earl, he derived political strength, not from the laws that governed his office, but from this enthusiastic personal loyalty.

When the oil and gas revenues slowed to a trickle, Edwards's political power waned as well. Edwards was fortunate that the big drop in oil prices occurred during the tenure of Republican governor Dave Treen, who was elected after the constitution prevented Edwards from serving a third term. Edwards easily defeated Treen in 1983 but was not able to reinvigorate the Louisiana economy without the oil and gas windfalls that he and his predecessors had used so effectively in the past. Edwards's power as governor was clearly related to his power to perform as a populist. That required resources. With the decline in oil and gas revenues, Louisiana did not have them. John Maginnis recognized that the dramatic drop in oil and gas prices would cause a seismic shift in the way Louisiana was governed. He underlined the point when he titled his insightful book on the 1983 Edwards-Treen election *The Last Hayride*.[13] After being saddled with two racketeering trials during that term, Edwards was not able to win reelection in 1987.

In that 1987 election several major political players, including three of the state's seven congressmen, challenged Edwards. His old ally, then-Democratic congressman Billy Tauzin, seemed a likely victor, but Tauzin's campaign fizzled to a fourth-place finish. Edwards's main Republican challenger was suburban New Orleans congressman Robert Livingston, who would eventually become chair of the House Appropriations Committee and almost Speaker of the House until he was toppled by disclosures about his marital infidelity in the midst of the Clinton impeachment trials. Secretary of State Jim Brown had won statewide office, but his campaign never took flight. Shreveport congressman Charles "Buddy" Roemer, probably the least known of the five main contenders, ran far back in the pack until near election day when his message of a "Roemer Revolution" began to resonate with voters. Shortly after he was endorsed by most of the major state newspapers, he pulled away from the pack and took the momentum going into the first election. His target was clearly Edwards: "The main issue in this campaign is Edwin Edwards. We've got to slay the dragon."[14] He did, temporarily. The final tally: Roemer 516,195, Edwards 437,801, Livingston 287,780, Tauzin 154,079, and Brown 138,223.

Edwards pulled out of the runoff race in the middle of the night, allowing Roemer to become governor—but denying him a chance to win with a majority mandate. That night Edwards said in defeat, "The Chinese have a saying that if you wait on the riverbank long enough, the bodies of all of your dead enemies will float by."[15] Perhaps he was hinting at Roemer's political career floating in that river.

Edwards made an improbable comeback in 1991 in the infamous runoff with David Duke but was never able to regain anything close to the power he had exercised in previous terms. Edwards was strong enough to run first, while the weakened incumbent Roemer, with whom the public had become disillusioned after he failed to bring many of his major campaign promises to fruition, finished third. Amidst a great deal of fanfare, especially emanating from his friend President George Bush, Roemer was the first sitting governor to switch parties, turning Republican. Although Roemer's ideology roamed somewhere between the two parties (he is a self-described social liberal and economic conservative), the party switch may have been as much political as ideological. Polls showed him vulnerable, and the move may have had as much to do with fending off mainstream Republican opposition as with a better ideological fit.

Edwards eventually won his fourth term but was not strong enough to do much else—and he didn't really seem to care. During the campaign he was asked, "Do you want to win this election to be governor or to beat Roemer?" Edwards answered that he wanted both and then added, "The best thing that can happen to me is to win this election and to die the next day."[16]

"Cut the Fat"?

A Mardi Gras parade in Louisiana is in many ways the embodiment of the relationship between a populist government and the people. In Huey Long's terms, the "haves" are redistributing wealth to the "have-nots." At a recent Mardi Gras parade in Baton Rouge, where in true Carnival spirit the elite were throwing trinkets to the masses, a state senator from the area was represented on the floats, as are most local politicians. His "throw"—as Mardi Gras trinkets are called—was a plastic cup advertising his next campaign. On it was a phrase that was completely antithetical to the parade and all that it stands for: "Cut the Fat!" The irony exemplified the Louisiana legislative dilemma. It is a history in which the governor gives and the legislature takes away.

The road to legitimacy for the Louisiana legislature has been a rocky one. The dominance of the governor in Louisiana is rooted not in constitutional powers but in a culture of personal power created and defined by Huey Long, Earl Long, and Edwin Edwards. Changing the culture is much more difficult than changing the rules. The lopsided relationship prevailed through much of the twentieth century.

The event that set the stage for the governor's dominance of the legislature was the impeachment of Huey Long in 1929. Huey realized that in order for the governor to be strong, the legislature must be weak—and that mindful manipulation of it must be an operating principle of the governor's office. The vote for impeachment in the Louisiana house of representatives was a call to arms for Long. Not only did he see to it that the possibility of conviction was dead on arrival in the Louisiana senate, but he purposefully and effectively controlled the legislature from that day forward.

The lesson of that impeachment was not lost on governors who followed. Periodic shows of strength by the legislature were normally quelled quickly by the governor for most of the remainder of the century. Some of the most notorious examples of a governor tyrannizing the legislature were found during the reign of Huey's brother Earl. Even though Earl Long was publicly embarrassed when he was sent away for psychological help after a rambling, profanity-laced tirade delivered before the Louisiana senate, he was able to dominate the legislature during most of his tenure.

Earl's political maneuvering was a clear indication of insight into the legislative process. He would pack with loyal lieutenants his favorite senate committee, the ambiguously named "Judiciary B" Committee, because most of the key details of legislation are hammered out in committee. He would often carefully steer his favorite projects through that committee to have them wrought into the shape he wanted before they arrived on the floor of the senate. The fact that the senate continues to use this traditional committee naming system is a fairly conscious symbolic reminder of Earl Long's scheming.

In Louisiana the basis of a governor's power was almost always political patronage—handing out jobs and pet projects for votes. The Louisiana culture created from abundant resources and a multiethnic setting made this political dynamic possible. It was much the same dynamic that allowed big-city mayors to wield overwhelming power in many other states during the same time. The Longs were often compared to big-city bosses like George Washington Plunkitt of the Tammany Hall machine in New York City, Mayor Richard Daley in Chicago, or Mayor E. H. Crump in Memphis. The Longs and Edwards were able to run an entire state with the same degree of coercion and the same tools as these men did in cities.

It is no surprise, then, that when the spotlight of public pressure turned on and against the city machines in the late 1960s, there was also public outcry for reform of the Louisiana legislature. Television, investigative journalism, and the successes of the social movements of the sixties put practitioners of "good-ole-boy" patronage politics under a media magnifying glass. This national phenomenon greased the wheels for a major reform movement in the Louisiana legislature. At the very least, the rules would change.

In the late 1960s and early 1970s, a group of legislators who called themselves "the Young Turks" spearheaded a dramatic wave of reform. They sought to overhaul the rules of engagement between the governor and the legislature. They wanted to give the legislature more credibility and leverage in the face of what had become a culture of gubernatorial dominance. The group was led by a young representative from Jonesboro in rural north Louisiana, E. L. "Bubba" Henry, who would eventually become speaker of the house and preside over the 1973 Louisiana constitutional convention. The group also included John Hainkel of New Orleans, who decades later became president of the Louisiana senate, and John Alario of Westwego, who would serve as speaker of the house.

This combination of the receptive times for reform and potent leadership led to a tremendous series of successes by the Young Turks. The committee system was streamlined and strengthened, making it more difficult for governors to use antics like those by which Earl Long manipulated the legislative process. The legislative research staff was given more resources as a counterbalance to the vast bureaucratic resource base that the governorship had at its disposal in the executive branch. A legislative

Fiscal Office was created that allowed the legislature to monitor the workings and oversee this vast executive bureaucracy. The presiding officers of each chamber, the speaker of the house and the president of the senate, were given much more concentrated power and independence in order to provide effective voices of opposition to the governor. By the early 1970s, after the current Louisiana constitution had gone into effect, the legislature, on paper, had become quite a formidable institution.

It is perhaps telling that almost all of these legislative reforms came with the blessing of the man who would become the most powerful governor in Louisiana in the late twentieth century, Edwin Edwards. Indeed most of the reforms were passed during the first years of Edwards's first term. Edwards, who obviously desired to be a strong governor, must have realized that the source of the governor's strength in Louisiana lies not in constitutional and statutory rules, but in the culture of gubernatorial dominance.

In the decades that followed the Young Turk reforms, the relationship between governor and legislature did slowly change, and the legislature did exert more power. The reforms themselves, however, were probably not the main cause of the change. Governor Edwards quickly adapted to the rules and in his first two terms was arguably as strong, powerful, and masterful in engineering legislative successes as Huey or Earl Long had ever been. Eventually, governors learned that the key to the manipulation of the legislature was in ensuring that political allies were elected to head each of the chambers, as speaker of the house and president of the senate. (In the middle of Buddy Roemer's four-year term, the Louisiana senate summarily replaced Roemer's choice for president of the senate with an ally of his supposedly vanquished opponent, Edwin Edwards.)

Gubernatorial control of the leadership positions in the halls of the legislature was not the only way in which governors sought to dominate legislative politics. Even though the legislature had created a strong structural organization with the Young Turk reforms, neither the house nor the senate has any strong political organization. Governors easily fill the vacuum by building coalitions for key pieces of legislation through promising to put favors in the governor's proposed budget.

In most states and in the United States Congress, the parties play a critical organizing role. By contrast, the structural weakness of the two-party system in Louisiana is obvious in the political behavior of the legislature. Individual legislators often loudly and proudly proclaim that they are their "own man" (or woman) and not beholden to any political party or group—and it shows. The president of the senate in another state told this author that he was shocked when he visited the Louisiana legislature and saw no visible signs of party organization or cohesion. Indeed, Republicans and Democrats alike hold top positions of leadership in both chambers, and neither party can claim any semblance of discipline, even on procedural votes. This lack of concerted effort allows the governor to be the principal organizing force in the legislature and is another way that governors can exert much more influence than the constitution would predict.

Still, even though recent governors have been adept at maneuvering their proposals through the legislature, a trend of decreasing gubernatorial dominance became evident in the 1980s and 1990s. As the price of oil and gas fell, the rapid dwindling of the state's financial resources made it much more difficult for governors to promise jobs or projects to legislators in exchange for their support for other proposals made by the governor. When the governor loses this political leverage, the culture of dominance breaks down.

Less than ten years after the cataclysmic plunge of petroleum prices, two conspicuous incidents signaled the governor's diminished influence in the legislature. In 1991, for the first time in at least seventy years (and probably since well before that), a governor's veto was overridden by the legislature. After several tries at compromise, Buddy Roemer's veto of a piece of antiabortion legislation was overturned in the house and in the senate. This historic override was a symptom of a struggle that had lasted most of Roemer's term, but the change cannot be attributed solely to Roemer. When Edwards succeeded Roemer two years later, Edwards had two of his vetoes overridden by the legislature as well. Indeed, during the 1980s and early 1990s, when the Louisiana economy was faring poorly, the influence of the governor over the legislature waned considerably. As the economy picked up in the late 1990s, Governor Foster was able to reestablish some of the dynamics that had favored the governor before the economic decline. When he ran for reelection in 1999, the Louisiana economy appeared to be on a sound footing.

Until the Louisiana legislature organizes itself politically, it is likely to play a secondary role to the governor and not radically change the dynamics dictated by the political culture. In good economic times, the governor can trade the carrot of perks, patronage, and programs to individual legislators and bargain together winning coalitions. In poor economic times, the legislature will more often than not let the governor make the tough, politically damaging decisions about where to cut programs or how to raise taxes.

The legislature's predicament was captured in the apparently unconsciously ironic political slogan on the Mardi Gras cup mentioned at the beginning of this section. State Senator Jay Dardenne is a poster boy for reform politics in Louisiana who went from being a self-described "grenade thrower" in the fourth Edwards administration to the ultimate insider in the Foster administrations, where he served as chair of the powerful Senate Finance Committee and as a legislative floor leader for the governor. Dardenne represents a significant force in Louisiana politics. Perhaps the legislature is changing. In that Baton Rouge Fat Tuesday parade, celebrating the archetypical Louisiana holiday for excess and sharing the wealth, it was Senator Dardenne's throw cup that proclaimed "Cut the Fat!"

The Interest in Legislative Parties

If the phrase "political party" is uttered in the Louisiana capitol, you can bet that it is a reference to an event, normally with seafood and beer, rather than to anything having to do with Democrats or Republicans. Legislators and legislative staffers alike can indulge in an almost daily series of distinctly Louisiana-style socials during any legislative session. After all, when the city of New Orleans or the Louisiana Seafood Industry throws a party, all but the most disciplined find the temptation hard to resist.

The importance of interest groups in Louisiana is much more than a superficial addition to the legislative party scene. Interest-group politics is tailor-made for the freewheeling Louisiana political culture. With the pronounced lack of Democratic and Republican Party institutional strength, interest groups find it fairly easy to fill the gaps in affecting legislation. Those spectacular parties are celebrating even more spectacular successes over the years.

The evidence of interest-group command in Louisiana politics is more than anecdotal. Academic studies confirm what appears to be unmistakable: Louisiana is a state where interest groups play a big role in legislative politics. Ronald Hrebenar and Clive Thomas have carried out a series of fifty state studies of the impact of interest groups in state politics. In the latest edition of their study, a 1998 update, Louisiana is one of twenty-five states where interest groups are considered "dominant/complementary"—the second-highest category, below Alabama, Florida, Nevada, South Carolina, and West Virginia. (See table 3-C, Appendix 2, for the full categorization of states.)

In *Interest Group Politics in the Southern States*, Hrebenar and Thomas also analyze individual states to find out which particular interest groups are dominant within each (see table 3-D).[17] Business in general has eclipsed labor organizations, including teacher organizations, in the past decade or so. The Louisiana Association of Business and Industry (LABI) has become the dominant player in campaign contributions and is the best-known single lobby group in the state. The Louisiana Association of Trial Lawyers has recently become the most publicized opponent of business interests, surpassing the AFL-CIO and other labor groups, who dominated the business opposition agenda in the mid-to-late twentieth century.

Nothing in Common: The Judicial System

Visitors to the state capitol in Baton Rouge are not normally allowed access to the fourth-floor complex that houses the office of the governor and his staff. If they were, they would likely notice that the office itself looks remarkably like a judicial chamber. Their intuition would be correct. It was designed to house a courtroom when there was an ill-fated attempt to move Louisiana's highest state court from New Orleans to the state capital (and state capitol). The appearance of the office of the governor as judge and jury is eye-catching and perhaps unintentionally symbolic. The Louisiana legal system is, like the governor, an abnormally political part of the government.

While the power of the governor in relation to the legislature is the most widely discussed manifestation of the Louisiana culture in its political institutions, the impact of the culture on the legal system is even more glaring. Most Louisianians know that their state's legal system is unique. But since lawyers and political scientists are about the only folks who make much of an effort to learn the intricacies of legal theory, the precise nature of the difference is not exactly common knowledge. When asked how it is different, the average Louisianian will answer with a confused mumble of a sentence in which the words "Napoleonic Code" figure prominently. As with most conventional wisdom about politics, the general instinct is correct, while the particulars are left wanting.

The Louisiana system is unlike any other in the United States because it is based on civil law. The legal systems in every other state court system and the legal system in the United States court system are based on common law. A civil law system is one in which judges make decisions based on a written code passed by the legislature. A common-law system is one in which judges base their decisions on other cases.

In Louisiana, the code passed and amended by the legislature over time was heavily influenced not only by the French Napoleonic Code, but Spanish civil law as well. Specific echoes of French and Spanish civil law remain highly significant in Louisiana in such areas as marriage and community property, but the deeper significance of this legal heritage is philosophical. To reiterate, the private legal system in Louisiana is based on code, rather than on common law. This broad characteristic, rather than the particulars of the rules, sets the entire Louisiana legal philosophy apart from that of the forty-nine common-law states.

Common law assumes that the society has a broadly held set of norms that can guide judges in making decisions. Thus judges make decisions based on how similar cases have been decided in the past, or judicial precedent. It is a system based on legal tradition. The volatile Louisiana culture makes it difficult for a common set of legal ideals to be defined. Although the sources of the law in a civil system include custom, such a system relies primarily on legislative code. The code itself is subject to the instability of the political culture. No dominant culture means no agreed-upon set of ideals and precedents upon which judges can make decisions.

The code system suits Louisiana well. Under this system legislators, not judges, lay out the rules, often in great detail, for deciding cases or controversies. Judges and lawyers must first consult the legislature-approved code before applying the law. Only if the code does not apply is the practice of reviewing precedent relevant.

The competitive, volatile Louisiana culture also underlies the second defining characteristic of the Louisiana court system—that all judges are elected. A state that does not trust judges to base decisions on other judges' decisions, but rather on legislative will, would also not be prone to allow judges to be appointed for lifetime terms. In Louisiana, interpretation of the law, like all other facets of government, is a political decision made by politically selected officials.

Melinda Gann Hall was interested in the question of the effect of elections on judicial decision-making and conducted in-depth interviews with the members of the Louisiana Supreme Court in 1983. Hall guaranteed complete confidentiality in order to solicit candid results. Her intriguing study spells out the precise effects of election on judicial decisions in the Louisiana Supreme Court. As she summarizes her findings:

> This look at the Louisiana Supreme Court presents some evidence that suggests that certain types of justices may, indeed, be affected by the pressures of re-election. Justices who find themselves in the court minority, who perceive themselves to have views inconsistent with those of their constituents, and who have very strong ambitions to retain their positions and fear electoral challenge, may be extremely hesitant to voice disagreement with the court's decisions on highly controversial issues of public policy. To avoid singling themselves out for criticism during the re-election process, these types of justices may suppress the expression of dissent. Whether voters and opponents are cognizant of the justices' behavior or not, certain justices seem to fear the prospect of electoral sanction and therefore alter their behavior.[18]

Judges altering their behavior because of the fear of electoral sanction is the inevitable outcome of election of judges. Yet the predicament is not a bad one if the enactment of the will of the people in the legal system is valued by the particular political culture. The value of "people's justice" seems to be unavoidable in a state where the culture is so competitive and volatile.

In Louisiana, the courts are obviously not immune to a prevailing culture that says all decisions are always up for grabs and always political. Both of the unique characteristics of the courts in the state epitomize the point. First, the Louisiana code law system, under which rules of judicial decisions are subject to legislative guidelines, is a recognition that even in the arena of the courts, governmental decisions are political. Second, not only do legislators tell judges how to decide cases, but the judges themselves are all elected. When judges are elected, their decisions will include political considerations.

Summing Up: Culture and the Basics of Government

The simple, basic building blocks of the Louisiana government, the governor, the legislature, and the courts are not simple or basic at all when compared to other states. On paper, the governor and the legislature appear to have a fairly checked and balanced relationship like that of most other states. In practice, the governor dominates.

The money that flowed from the Louisiana oil, gas, and petrochemical base allowed Governor Huey Long to hand out projects and patronage at will to individual legislators and piece together winning coalitions when he needed them. His brother Earl continued the tradition of gubernatorial power and was equally adept at manipulating the legislative process to his advantage. Toward the end of the twentieth century, the third master-politician governor, Edwin Edwards, even allowed the legislature to pass a series of reforms designed to strengthen its hand against him, but he continued to prevail because the state had the resources and he had the political skill to use those resources to his advantage.

The legislature has tried to reform itself several times and was most successful in the early 1970s when a group of self-described "Young Turks" took advantage of a reform fever sweeping the nation and passed a dramatic series of rules changes that gave much greater structural strength to both the house of representatives and the senate. When oil-and-gas-related resources waned in the 1980s, these reforms and the economic climate allowed the legislature to assert itself so much that in 1991 it actually overturned a governor's veto.

In other words, when the first hallmark of the Louisiana culture, an abundance of money from natural resources, subsides, the governor loses some strength. The prospects of legislative power over the governor are definitely helped when the state economy is in a slump and the governor cannot use his political skill to consistently build winning coalitions by promising jobs and projects for districts.

But even in poor economic times, the legislature is hampered by the other feature of the Louisiana culture—the volatile and almost anarchic political structure. Strong political parties would benefit the legislature in bargaining with the governor, but the culture of the state does not well support such well-defined political institutions as political parties. Until substantial groups of legislators adopt a "United We Stand, Divided We Are Eaten Alive by the Governor" attitude and organize themselves politically, the legislature itself will remain an underdog in most fights with the governor. Since most Louisianians and probably most legislators prefer the present situation, that is not likely to happen.

Finally, while the role of money from natural resources figures prominently in the ebb and flow of the legislature/governor relationship, it is the multiethnic part of the Louisiana culture that has the most profound impact on the third major governmental institution, the courts. The Louisiana judicial system is unlike any other in the United States because it does not adhere solely to the principles of common law. Rather, it is rooted in a code law system that acknowledges that no one set of values is ever agreed upon and all decisions—even those made by a judge in a case concerning two private individuals—are political.

Huey Long leading the Louisiana State University marching band. Legend has it that when Huey was felled by an assassin's bullet, his last words were, "What will my poor boys at LSU do without me?"

Huey Pierce Long Photograph, MSS 2906, Louisiana and Lower Mississippi Valley Collections, LSU Libraries, Louisiana State University

Earl Long on the stump. The men on the stand with Uncle Earl are Jimmie Davis and Bill Dodd.

Langston McEachern, photographer; Shreveport Times *Collection, Noel Memorial Library Archives, LSU in Shreveport*

Blaze Starr, the Bourbon Street stripper who was Earl Long's paramour.

James Terry

Leander Perez, the rabidly right-wing segregationist and political boss of Plaquemines Parish.

The Louisiana Collection, State Library of Louisiana, Baton Rouge

Dave Treen, the first Republican governor of Louisiana since Reconstruction.

James Terry

Ernest “Dutch” Morial, mayor of New Orleans and the first black elected to Louisiana’s legislature in modern times.

James Terry

John Breaux, longtime U.S. senator noted for his ties to both parties in Washington.

Robert Mann

Edwin Edwards with wife Candy in happy times long before Edwards's conviction on federal racketeering charges.

James Terry

David Duke, Klansman turned politician, pressing the flesh during his 1991 run for governor.

Philip Gould

Mike Foster, a popular conservative Republican who served two terms as governor.

James Terry

Charles "Buddy" Roemer, the governor who switched from Democrat to Republican while in office, only to lose his bid for reelection.

James Terry

Mary Landrieu, the first woman elected to the U.S. Senate from Louisiana.

James Terry

B. B. "Sixty" Rayburn, a powerhouse in the Louisiana state senate for more than forty years, confers with Cleo Fields, who when elected at age twenty-four was the youngest state senator in Louisiana history.

James Terry

U.S. Representative William Jefferson, who lost the 1999 Louisiana gubernatorial race to Mike Foster in a vote divided sharply along racial lines.

James Terry

Kathleen Babineaux Blanco, elected in 2003 as Louisiana's first female governor.

Jay Faugot Photography

4. Local Politics

All Politics Is Not Local

"All politics is local" is the legendary axiom of former U.S. Speaker of the House Thomas "Tip" O'Neill. In Louisiana, however, the axiom does not fit. All politics is not local because state politics invades almost every phase of local politics.

Courts routinely remind local governments of the judicial precedent commonly called "Dillon's Rule," which makes it very clear that when push comes to shove, local governments are absolute creatures of the state government. In Louisiana, where state politics is always competitive and unstable, local governments, local politicians, and local campaigns often find themselves at the mercy of state political shenanigans. When politics is one continuous, exhausting game of King-of-the-Hill, as it is in Louisiana, winners of the moment will try to spread their tentacles as completely and substantially as possible; local politics and government are always vulnerable to some unexpected, often absurd intrusion by the latest state winning team.

The vulnerability of local politics does not always derive from straightforward state intrusion. Parish governments and municipal governments know that they are creatures of the state, and they often act accordingly whether there is obvious intrusion or not. All local governments were created by the state of Louisiana and all are nurtured by it. It shows.

Parish governments were designed simply to be the administrators of state policy. However, as this chapter will illustrate, parish politicians can take a cue from their creators in state government and build very substantial bases of power. Leander Perez of Plaquemines Parish was an example of what can be done with the nominal resources of parish government in the fertile political culture of Louisiana. His exceptional career provides a particularly instructive case of a parish official amassing dictatorial power with little official authority.

City governments *in* Louisiana are also distinctly city governments *of*

Louisiana. The big-city politics of New Orleans reflects the constant battles for dominance that characterize the state. Even in the medium-sized cities of Baton Rouge and Shreveport politicians have obviously learned their trade from the teachers in state government.

This chapter will show that local politics in Louisiana has a distinctively statewide tenor. The competitiveness and lack of a dominant political culture in the state as a whole certainly seem to have pervaded local governments' activity. Sometimes, however, the effect of state politics on local governance is more direct. The examples of direct statewide meddling into local politics are legendary.

After Earl Long was elected governor in 1948, he severely punished his New Orleans enemies in a vendetta that Robert Mann details in his biography of Earl's nephew Russell Long: "By the time Earl finished bludgeoning the city, New Orleans bore 25 percent of the state's total tax burden, yet received less than 10 percent of the revenues. Another bill Earl rammed through the legislature gave the governor total control over the appointment of all New Orleans Dock Board commissioners, robbing [political enemy and mayor Chep] Morrison of important patronage. Earl also persuaded legislators to modify the composition of city government, further weakening the mayor's appointive powers."[1]

Earl Long's penchant for meddling in the affairs of local government to reward friends and punish enemies was so blatant that it shamed the legislature into passing the Lawrason Act. Before this act, municipalities could apply for special charters whereby the legislature would determine unique sets of rules that did everything from setting limits on taxing and borrowing to prescribing forms of government. The negotiations for liberal rules by local officials with the governor and legislature were legendary and provided a smorgasbord of opportunities for everything from petty political payoffs to bribery and corruption.

The Lawrason Act represented an attempt to change all of that. It prescribed that rules governing municipalities were to be determined by their population. The most egregious victim (and sometimes beneficiary) of state interference in local politics, however, found little relief in the new legislation. Since New Orleans is easily the most populous city in Louisiana, even under the Lawrason Act it is in a category all its own, and all the rules governing the city apply to it alone.

Power Politics in the Parishes

As with political power relationships between cities and the state, the influence of state government over parish governments is not left to accident or interpretation. On paper, the power appears to flow absolutely and resolutely in one direction—from the state to the parish. Every Louisiana constitution, including the present one, makes it clear that parish governments are designed to be merely administrative units of the state. The state government makes the decisions, the parish governments carry them out.

For example, although parish school boards have nominal control over many more personnel and much more money than any other local governing body, the decisions and the majority of the funds flow from above. Other functions of local government are carried out by distinct, disconnected parish offices such as sheriff, tax assessor, and state constable. All are elected (of course), and the head of each can form a distinct political base that may be, in turn, courted by legislators and statewide elected officials.

Of course not all parish officials have the reputation for functioning merely as loyal minions of the state, determined to carry out programs honestly, impartially, and efficiently. Fairly or not, two groups of parish officials tend to raise the most eyebrows when "good government" types and investigative reporters start poking around the parish seats: sheriffs and district attorneys. Their duties are clear enough. Sheriffs collect taxes and put people in jail. District attorneys (who are categorized in the constitution as parish-level officials but in some cases actually cover two or three parishes) are the district court prosecutors for the state. Candidates for governor or almost any statewide office usually actively solicit support from the "courthouse gangs" of district attorneys and sheriffs.

Why, then, do sheriffs and district attorneys have an aura of political power? The answer becomes readily apparent at a Louisiana Sheriffs' Association meeting. The quiet informal conversations reveal how well these parish officials know state officials. To an outside observer, the casual familiarity might seem odd. However, many Louisiana sheriffs and district attorneys are extremely well connected to state politicians because they have day-to-day contact and access to the most powerful people in any community. They are on the front lines every day.

Although the Louisiana population is disproportionately poor and disproportionately incarcerated, it is the relationships that sheriffs and district attorneys build with the wealthy and well established that bring them power. Wealthy business owners, established (or entrenched) families, local leaders, and state politicians all can have their careers ruined by even the hint of personal or family scandal or impropriety. The simple perception that sheriffs and district attorneys have some discretion in deciding whether to pursue leads or tips that could result in investigations of those who have the most to lose is the source of enormous power.

While powers of this sort are hardly unique to Louisiana, the way they are used here is perhaps intensified by the state's competitive political culture. The perception of power among the local business, social, and political leaders stirs considerable interest in the offices of sheriff and district attorney among ambitious state politicians. Simply put, state politicians think that sheriffs and district attorneys can deliver votes.

Leander Perez: Making George Wallace Seem "Like an Angel"

As with the governor's office, local political power in Louisiana arises not from the institution itself but from personal manipulation of its formal duties. Some of the most notoriously powerful politicians statewide in Louisiana have been local government officials. Probably the best known was Plaquemines Parish district attorney Leander Perez.

Perhaps no other tract of land in the continental United States is as isolated from civilization as the farthest reaches of southeastern Louisiana. More than half of Plaquemines Parish is under water with more and more land succumbing to the Gulf of Mexico every day.[2] The Mississippi River is as much a part of the life of Plaquemines Parish as streets and avenues are to the urban centers of the northeast, and many of the homes in the parish can only be reached by watercraft. The parish has a rich history as one of the leading trapping, fishing, and hunting areas in all of North America. Out of this remoteness emerged the most infamous Louisiana local leader of the twentieth century.

Perez used political cunning and geographic isolation from the rest of Louisiana and the United States to build a fiefdom that eventually made him one of the richest men in Louisiana. Furthermore, his political and economic successes gave him a platform from which to launch campaigns against integration that made "Governor George Wallace of Alabama

[seem] like an angel of reason and moderation and ex-Governor Ross W. Barnett of Mississippi a towering intellect."[3]

Perez was notorious for using inventive ways to deliver votes to candidates for parish, state, and even national office, and he exchanged these votes for favors in the parish, in Baton Rouge, and in Washington. "Judge" Perez, as he was called for decades, found ways through his position as district attorney in Plaquemines to skim the profits of the productive oil and sulfur industries within the parish, making him a very rich man while keeping his fellow citizens poor and uneducated.

While Perez's story is like that of many twentieth-century southern politicians, it is also very different because Perez did not aspire to be anything more than a local politician. Unlike Strom Thurmond of South Carolina and George Wallace of Alabama, both of whom Perez emulated and influenced, he never felt compelled to advance to state or national politics through a gubernatorial or congressional election.

Instead, Perez created in his own small section of the state a political fortress ruled by him and him alone. He held sole power over Plaquemines's populace, its laws, and perhaps most important, its mineral resources, and he was virtually impervious to any other contenders for this power. Through his absolute control over one small piece of Louisiana, Leander Perez was often able to force Louisiana politicians at every level to concede economic and political favors to him. His was one of the most influential and longest-running political machines in Louisiana history.

After graduating from Louisiana State University in Baton Rouge and then Tulane University Law School in New Orleans, Perez began practicing law in New Orleans while retaining a residence in Plaquemines, a setup that was ideal for his political aspirations. He ran for the state house of representatives in 1916, campaigning against the ruling boss in the parish. Perez received only about a dozen votes and lost the election.

After a brief training stint during World War I (he saw no action and was never sent overseas), Perez returned to Plaquemines and a twist of fate landed him his first political office. After the drowning death of Judge Robert Hingle, who held jurisdiction over both Plaquemines and St. Bernard Parishes, Governor Ruffin G. Pleasant asked Governor-elect John Parker to recommend an appointee to fill the remainder of Hingle's term. Parker selected Perez for little more reason than that the young lawyer had opposed the anti-Parker ruling elite in 1916. However, since the judgeship was an elective office, just being appointed by the governor did not ensure that Perez would be in the job very long.

Shortly thereafter Perez ran for the office and narrowly won a full term to the bench. He immediately set out to dismantle the ruling political ring in Plaquemines and St. Bernard Parishes. He began by influencing the selection of the grand jury for the district, thereby guaranteeing that those he wanted indicted would be indicted and that his political allies would not. He had the voting registrar indicted for bypassing areas that were known to oppose the sitting political machine. Perez then moved to win votes in the trapping community, a large portion of Plaquemines voters, by ruling in their favor in a case where the opposing landowners were represented by John Dymond. Dymond was the leader of the political machine that Perez wished to dismantle. Perez knew how to use his power to gain more power.

Political squabbling continued in the district when the district attorney, a former Perez backer named Philip R. Livaudais, attempted to prosecute several suspects in the "rum-running" murders of two sheriff's deputies. When some of Perez's friends and political allies were implicated, he chose to set the trial dates of seven murder cases on the same day, leaving the frustrated district attorney with no time to prepare a case. Altogether, forty prosecution cases were discontinued. Some of those set free without trial went on to political office alongside Perez.[4]

After the frustrations of the "rum murders," those opposing Judge Perez, led by Livaudais, convened and signed a petition of impeachment in an attempt to put an end to Perez before his power was solidified in the district. Despite the serious offenses noted in the petition, including Perez's insistence on possessing a pearl-handled revolver while presiding over court, he defended himself by portraying his opponents as puppets of the Dymond machine.

As closing arguments were set to begin before the Louisiana Supreme Court, the attorneys returned to the courtroom after a meeting in chambers and announced that all charges against the judge had been dropped. One of the most sensational trials in state history ended in what amounted to a cease-fire. Both sides apologized in the press about unfortunate things said in the trial and during their political squabbles. With his survival as judge intact, Leander Perez set his sights on becoming the absolute political power in the region.

The Democratic primary of 1924 was to be the ultimate showdown between the "Old Regulars" led by Dymond and Livaudais and the "New Regulars" led by Perez and his friend Claude Meraux. Perez actually ran for district attorney while allowing Meraux the chance to succeed him on the bench. New Regulars won almost every seat, thanks in part to the fact that the Old Regular voter registrar had been disposed of by Perez. The new order had come to power in Plaquemines and St. Bernard Parishes, and state politicians in New Orleans and elsewhere realized that they had a new force to deal with in the southern part of the state. However, no one knew to what extent that force would wield its power for the next half-century.

After establishing his political preeminence in Plaquemines/St. Bernard, Perez quickly began to increase his own wealth by manipulating his constituents and by taking advantage of his office, practices that would continue until his death. The first example of this was dubbed the "trappers' war." The mid-1920s amounted to a minor golden age for south Louisiana muskrat trappers—and a golden opportunity for Perez. As legal adviser for the St. Bernard Trappers' Association, Perez enriched himself through double-dealing involving landownership and trapping rights on some 100,000 acres. At one point some of the trappers became so outraged that he crossed the Mississippi in a rowboat in order to escape their wrath. He survived, but at least one man was killed in the turmoil surrounding the district attorney's machinations.

The second of Perez's little wars occurred in the 1940s during the climax of tensions between Huey Long's followers and those who detested the assassinated governor and senator. When the reformist and anti-Long candidate Sam Jones won the governor's race in 1940, one of his first acts was to set up a Crime Commission responsible for eliminating political crooks and corruption throughout the state. Perez was high on their list. The commission went after the financial books of the companies that profited most from Plaquemines's and St. Bernard's mineral wealth, suspecting correctly that Perez was behind the skimming of profits. Perez tied up the investigation with a series of legal obstacles, including numerous countersuits.

The conflict between the two intensified when Jones set out to replace the deceased sheriff of Plaquemines Parish. Since the duties of the sheriff included collecting taxes in the parish, even an interim sheriff from the opposition posed a dangerous threat to the Perez regime. Jones appointed his man and promptly asked for the tax books. Perez refused to hand them over and began organizing the Plaquemines Parish Wartime Emergency Patrol, supposedly to protect the coastline from German submarines. Actually, Jones was threatening to send the State Guard to Plaquemines to take the tax records, and Perez hoped the Parish Patrol would supply the armed strength to prevent this. Jones responded by declaring martial law in the parish. As the State Guard marched on the courthouse in the parish seat, the Perez faction faded and the district attorney himself again fled across the river, after destroying records that might incriminate him. Yet when the normally scheduled election was held for sheriff following this comic-opera debacle, Perez's candidate emerged victorious.

That was the pattern for much of Perez's career. Despite the efforts of the occasional reform governor—and even distinctly nonreform governors such as Earl Long, after the two had a falling-out in the late 1940s—the boss of Plaquemines did largely what he wanted in his isolated domain.

One thing he did exceedingly well was to make money. Since the land was covered in swamps, dense forests, and blackwater bayous, much of it was still owned by the state. Seeing no use for these inhospitable tracts, the state regularly granted thousands of acres to local levee boards and school boards. As the center of the local political machine, Leander Perez controlled the levee board that controlled the land. His position also allowed him to be the first in the parish to hear of interest in any parcel of land from, say, an outside oil company. He created phony land companies to buy such tracts cheap from the unsuspecting (save Perez) levee board, then sold them to the interested parties for ten times the price paid. He was never on record as the chief shareholder or owner of these profitable dummy land companies. Instead he charged the companies, whose corporate offices were the same as his offices, enormous legal fees for his work as their attorney.

Any opposition to this system was overshadowed by the fact that Perez's allies, many of whom also had interests in the enterprise, were in charge of almost every local government office. Any oil company that refused to do business with Perez in essence refused to do business in Plaquemines.[5]

Perez manipulated other industries in the parish as well. After geologists discovered the second-largest sulphur deposit in the world below the muddy soil of Plaquemines, companies were eager to stake claim to Perez's fiefdom. Perez greeted them with the same tactics he had used with the oil companies—and a few new tactics as well. When seven hundred acres of land came up for auction because of unpaid taxes, law required that the sale be advertised to the public. Perez influenced the local newspaper editor. The sale was indeed advertised—but the 100 copies of the special edition containing the notice were not distributed until six weeks after the land had been sold to a Perez associate. When the papers were entered into the sheriff's files as proof of advertisement, no one asked any questions.

Perez even attempted to redraw the borders of some towns for his financial advantage. Noting the discrepancy in the amount of land granted to a local levee board during and outside of the flood seasons, Perez sued for disputed land. Because of the volatile nature of the Mississippi and its effect on the surrounding townships, the courts often had difficulty deciding who owned plots of land that might be worth a million dollars apiece. By manipulating this indecision, along with using questionable surveys and disputed maps, Perez was able to increase his fortune deal by deal.[6]

Despite all of his questionable activities within Plaquemines and Louisiana, Leander Perez was most notorious outside the state for his ideas about racial segregation. At a dinner given in his honor in 1954, Perez declared war on integrationists in the South and elsewhere by stating that his final career goal would be to ensure the segregation of races. He researched the issue intensely, searching for any evidence that might prove his theory that blacks were inherently less intelligent than whites. He amassed outdated anthropological and social data as "proof" for his attacks, which portrayed blacks as primarily sexually driven animals who cost white taxpayers millions of dollars annually by procreating and filling up government housing projects. He believed that his campaign was to deliver whites from the burden of subsidizing blacks. Even more dire was any prospect of racial mixture. "God save America from a mongrelized race," he once intoned before a congressional committee.

Perez regarded African Americans as too dim even to understand their involvement in what he saw as the moral erosion of the country. Delving into a kind of neo-McCarthyism, he blamed Communists for the push for integration. He furthered his attack by castigating Jews as the driving force behind the Communist conspiracy.[7] The 1954 Supreme Court decision in *Brown v. Board of Education of Topeka* predictably outraged him: It showed, he said, how high the Communists had infiltrated the federal government. In a speech to a "leadership meeting" in Biloxi, Mississippi, he blasted the justices of the High Court as "nine pitiful, treasonable men" and the NAACP as a pro-Communist organization run by Jews. In the same speech Perez characterized the struggle of blacks against the violent oppression of whites as a component of the "proletarian revolution in America against Capitalism." The only resistance to this underground revolution, he proclaimed, was white solidarity. Whites must stop running away from Negroes and confront them head-on. It was the duty of the people of the South to save the Constitution and defy what the rest of the country might push on them: "if constitutional government is to be saved in this country, it will have to be saved by the Southern States."[8]

Perez's astounding accusations about African Americans and Communist conspiracy earned him the contempt of most of the country. However, segregationist groups hailed him as a hero and a champion of the white cause. He even received a plaque from the New Orleans Citizens' Council for his efforts on behalf of segregation. He also put his racist rhetoric into action. He refused to desegregate Plaquemines's schools, costing the parish $200,000 in federal funds in 1965.[9]

As a parish politician, Leander Perez amassed phenomenal power in the state and influence in the nation's segregation wars. When he died of a heart attack at the age of seventy-seven in 1969, his funeral was attended by governors (including George Wallace), judges, and dignitaries from across the South and the nation.[10]

Feeding the Sacred Cow

The power of Leander Perez was exceptional, but other parish officials have certainly had an impact on state politics. For example, most governors and state legislators over the years have understood that no matter how many political "revolutions" are called for and no matter how many sweeping reforms are proposed, no set of political initiatives can include any hint of a reduction in Louisiana's generous homestead exemption, which for many homeowners results in exceptionally low property taxes. Homestead exemption appears to be the single, inalterable "sacred cow" of state politics—and the credit for its status as such is usually given to a parish official, former Jefferson Parish assessor Lawrence Chehardy. When, in March 2000, Loyola University political science professor Edward Renwick compiled a list (see table 4-A, Appendix 1) for *Louisiana Life* magazine of "the twenty key people who have, for better or worse, influenced public policy in Louisiana during the two decades of this magazine's existence,"[11] Chehardy had the distinction of being the only parish official named. (The list did not extend back to the time of Leander Perez, who would certainly have qualified for it otherwise.) As Renwick explained his choice, Chehardy

> was successful in getting a $50,000 homestead exemption for homeowners in Louisiana while serving as assessor. In 1975, the elder Chehardy did not file for re-election. Instead, his 22-year-old son succeeded his father as the spokesman for the homestead exemption and was successful in raising it to $75,000. The homestead exemption is the sacred cow of Louisiana politics. Voters like it; the press, business and reformers do not. Business groups argue that the Louisiana tax structure, including the homestead exemption, is biased against business, leaving business to pick up the tab. The voters, however, appear to be very receptive to having business pay the bill.[12]

Governor Mike Foster—a pro-business governor if ever there was one—nevertheless responded to any cries for change in the homestead exemption with exactly that logic. On several occasions Foster called for a complete overhaul of the state's tax system, but almost always with the proviso that the homestead exemption stay untouched because it helps individuals and moves some of the burden for funding state government to businesses. The assessors have made their point, and this is one instance where local officials have played an enormous role in state politics and state policy.

Louisiana: The "Promised Land" for Reform?

In the mid-1960s there was a general, and very loud, cry for "reform" all over the country, especially in big cities where traditional political bosses were not wearing well under the gaze of television cameras and the pressure of civil rights legislation.

In part this also had to do with national trends in government. With the advent of the Great Society programs, government grew at all levels.

States recognized that counties, or in Louisiana's case parishes, were making more decisions in implementing more and more government programs. As the number of programs grew, local authorities by default gained increasing control over them because the states simply did not have the resources to micromanage them (despite the fantasies of state level politicians). States often helped, if not forced, local governments to change from administrative bodies to policy-making bodies.

Louisiana was a participant in that evolution. In fact, in 1975, University of New Orleans political science professor Richard Engstrom was so optimistic about reform in the parishes that he wrote an article for *Louisiana History* titled "Home Rule in Louisiana—Could This Be the Promised Land?"[13]

Many parishes, and certainly most rural parishes, have elected to continue using the century-old "police jury" system. Parishes are divided into wards, with each ward represented by a single police juror. The police juror sees to it that his or her ward has the necessary public facilities and that governmental programs are implemented in it. Roads are maintained, bridges are built, courthouses and prisons are run.

About one-third of the parishes in the state, however, especially in urban and suburban areas, and particularly in populous south Louisiana, have abandoned the standard police jury system in favor of a variety of other forms of government allowed by the state constitution, such as the council-manager system.

Similarly, change has trickled down to municipal governments. The three largest Louisiana cities, New Orleans, Baton Rouge, and Shreveport, all implemented major city and/or parish reforms well before the national reform movement caught steam. This perhaps very realistic view of reform and a "businesslike" approach to government is magnified by several "firsts" in Louisiana local government. New Orleans was one of the first cities in the country to completely consolidate its city and county (parish) government. As early as 1948, Baton Rouge pioneered a city-parish consolidation plan that was followed by similar landmark reforms in Nashville, Jacksonville, and Indianapolis. In the 1960s Shreveport switched to a commission form of government and was one of the very few large cities in the United States to adopt this innovative approach to city management.

On the face of it these three cities present textbook examples of cutting-edge municipal and local reforms. Technically, Louisiana has been ahead of the curve in reform government. But only technically. In Louisiana, "reform" is treated like just another coalition, just another way to win.

New Orleans and the Mardi Gras Syndrome

The concept of the "Mardi Gras syndrome" is a useful way to understand New Orleans's stunted growth in the last two hundred years. As the largest inland port in the nation, New Orleans seemed poised to become one of the three or four major commercial centers in the United States. Somehow, it has trouble moving out of the thick mud of the Mississippi River. New Orleans lags behind not only New York, Chicago, and Los Angeles, but also Houston, Atlanta, Dallas, and perhaps even Charlotte and Nashville as a major commercial hub for the region. Mardi Gras logic may well be the answer.

The New Orleans political culture is like the Louisiana political culture in that it is a culture of competing groups that work hard to keep control. Mardi Gras began as a festival wherein elite groups form private, exclusive krewes, parade in the streets, hide their faces behind masks, and throw trinkets to the screaming poorer masses.

The most common sight in the month-long festival is that of drunken crowds yelling "Throw me something, mista!" and fighting to grab plastic beads. The spectacle of gaudy, colorful, and essentially worthless trinkets being tossed to commoners by aristocrats who hide their identities carries almost too much symbolism to be taken seriously. I, like most Louisianians, love it—if, of course, we don't think about it *too* much.

As Tulane anthropologist Munro Edmonson observes, "There aren't many American festivals that could be described as congruent with the city they take place in. By analyzing the volunteer network that runs the Tournament of Roses, for instance, a social scientist might learn a bit about the pecking order of the more prosperous residents of Pasadena, but the participants in the central event—like the participants in the central event of the Indianapolis 500 or the Kentucky Derby—come from out of town."[14]

In *Lords of Misrule: Mardi Gras and the Politics of Race in New Orleans*, James Gill provides a comprehensive overview of the history of Mardi Gras, detailing the ties between the city's rising and falling elites and Mardi Gras.[15] Gill tells a tale of a politics dominated by ruling elites and reflected in the city's signature event. Gill's history of the connection between Mardi

Gras and city power is worth briefly summarizing here.

For over a hundred years preceding recent changes, New Orleans and Mardi Gras were dominated by a ruling elite that had been in the area almost since the founding of the city in 1718. In fact, the original party of French and French-Canadian colonists of Louisiana made their first landfall on Fat (Shrove) Tuesday in 1699. Their first camp was even named Pointe du Mardi Gras and was located seventy miles downriver from where New Orleans sits today. Tradition has it that the first Carnival balls were held in the late 1700s as pre-Lenten festivities. These society parties were the forerunner to what would become the Carnival season.

After the Louisiana Purchase by the United States from Napoleonic France in 1803, the Carnival balls and dance halls of New Orleans became scenes of ethnic friction between New Orleanians of French and Spanish heritage, called Creoles, and the newly arrived Americans. In 1827, again according to tradition, a group of Creole students fresh from Paris brought back to Louisiana a new Mardi Gras custom—dressing up extravagantly and dancing in the streets. Masked balls were scheduled by the Creole elite, while the public halls sufficed for those of the lesser classes. Early on, Mardi Gras segregated the different social levels in New Orleans.

Creole influence faded as Americans established their supremacy in the city. Other immigrants flooded into the bustling port as well. The influx of visitors that Mardi Gras brought with it, the rowdy behavior of both locals and outsiders, and the decay of any Creole or American leadership in the planning of the festival brought calls for its demise in 1856. It was at this juncture that a group of thirteen young men, only one of them bearing a French name, met in the Club Room in New Orleans to form the Gem Saloon Committee. This committee created what is now the oldest and most prestigious Carnival organization, the "Mistick Krewe of Comus," and revolutionized Mardi Gras forever. The krewe's first parade, in 1857, featured black men waving flambeaux, and it proceeded for two hours toward the Gaiety Theatre, where a ball was held late into the evening. This procession established the protocol by which all other Mardi Gras krewes and parades would be measured.

The ties between the elite and powerful of New Orleans and Comus were a sign of things to come. The city's mayor, Charles Waterman, was a member of Comus and made sure that the streets were cleared for the parade. The krewe evolved into the Pickwick Club, which joined the older

Boston Club as the two most elite social networks in New Orleans. Thus was forged the bond between the social elite and Mardi Gras. Comus grew year by year and its parade became the most anticipated event of the Carnival season. This was the state of Mardi Gras when war came to the city in 1861.

The Civil War affected the city and Mardi Gras immensely. Festivities were canceled from 1862 to 1865, and many of the original signatories of the Pickwick Club charter were killed or wounded in the fighting. Union troops seized New Orleans in the spring of 1862 and occupied the city for the rest of the war. The resentment toward Union occupation and the reins of Reconstruction, from which Louisiana was the last state to be released, cemented a retaliatory mood in New Orleans against blacks and all non-Anglo-Saxons. This mood would later be evident in the exclusionary actions made by the city's leaders and Mardi Gras krewes.

After Reconstruction two new groups arrived on the Mardi Gras scene. The addition of the "Ball of the Two Well-Known Gentlemen," established in 1884, gave the pimps and prostitutes of the city an outlet through which to join the elite of New Orleans in Carnival celebration. This ball became an annual social occasion for many city and state leaders who publicly accepted bribes for ignoring the behavior in "Storyville," the nickname given to the city's legally recognized red-light district. It was also during this time that the first organized group of black revelers joined the festivities. For decades blacks had been part of the Carnival processions dressed as wild Indians or carrying torches for the all-white krewes. However, during the long run of Buffalo Bill's Wild West show in the Crescent City, blacks were inspired by the show's black cowboys and Plains Indians to form a group dubbed the Creole Wild West Tribe. The tribe remains in existence today.

The Creole Wild West tribe is one of the many surviving Mardi Gras Indian tribes in New Orleans. The tradition of blacks dressing up as Indians can be dated to the late 1700s. The early French colonists in Louisiana attempted to enslave some of the Indians who lived there, but the natives' vast knowledge of the landscape made escape relatively easy for them. Thus, the French began to import African slaves. The Africans and Indians quickly bonded with each other due to the fact that they shared the same oppressor; consequently, the Indians began aiding the African slaves in their escape plans. "In 1746 archives begin to refer to slaves dressing as

Indians as the African Americans began to celebrate Mardi Gras."[16]

The turn of the century brought little change in the status quo of Mardi Gras or the politics of New Orleans. The ruling whites of the state and city seemed bent on preventing blacks from becoming a major political force, as their numbers would have allowed. The Louisiana Constitutional Convention of 1898 was called with its primary purpose being "to eliminate from the electorate the mass of corrupt and illiterate voters who have during the last quarter century degraded our politics." Not only blacks but also poor whites were targeted. The state's voter rolls shrank dramatically almost overnight.

It was at this pivotal time in Louisiana history, when African Americans were in a political and social climate that precluded any hint of equality, much less integration, with white society, that an all-black krewe by the name of Zulu began to parade the streets of New Orleans. The krewe grew out of an older social context in the black community. Since blacks could not count on the help of local or state government, or in many cases of the services of the white private sector, they had to provide certain basic social and economic services themselves. "The earliest signs of organization came from the fact that the majority of these men [the founders of Zulu] belonged to a Benevolent Aid Society. Benevolent Societies were the first forms of insurance in the black community where, for a small amount of dues, members received financial help when sick or financial aid when burying deceased members."[17]

Festivities were canceled again after the United States entered World War I in 1917. (That same year the Department of the Navy successfully pressured the city to close down the officially regulated prostitution business in Storyville.) Prohibition followed, and the Mardi Gras parades of Comus and Momus were slow to revive. Rex was the only krewe to parade in 1920, at least theoretically without the usual additive of alcohol. Mardi Gras historians universally regard that season as the most boring in Carnival history.

The gubernatorial election of 1928 brought to power Huey Long, whose populist "Every Man a King" platform of helping the poor by taxing the rich presented a clear threat to the New Orleans elite. Long berated them as being more concerned about their society balls and their parades than the plight of their fellow citizens. Snubbed by all of the New Orleans krewes during the Mardi Gras season following his election, Long became the first post-Reconstruction governor to receive no invitations to the balls. Long retaliated in 1930 by overrunning the city during Carnival and having dinner with ex-president Calvin Coolidge in a local hotel. He hoped to divert press away from the festivities with this self-described meeting between "the ex-president and the future president." His administration and those Longite administrations that would follow him drained funds from New Orleans to provide for social programs throughout the state.

Mardi Gras festivities were again curtailed by war after Pearl Harbor, and no parades rolled from 1942 until 1946. The years following the war, however, brought world-famous guests to the city, including native jazz legend Louis Armstrong and former king Edward VIII of England. A new period began in history that would bring enormous change to America and New Orleans.

The U.S. Supreme Court's decision in the *Brown v. Board of Education* case galvanized Louisiana segregationists to resist change. It also led to further federal court decisions directing the state to integrate its schools and public places. Would desegregation and the civil rights movement change New Orleans? Some thought it might not. As Lisa Baker suggests in the beginning of her book recounting school desegregation in New Orleans, aptly titled *The Second Battle of New Orleans* (1996), the city had a reputation for tolerance: "As a testing ground for school desegregation, it seemed about right. It appeared to lack the rigidity of Montgomery or Memphis, to have, on the surface, the least Southern mind set of any deep South city, its mixed cultural heritage offering the best conditions for social change, even change involving so long settled a matter as relations between the races."[18]

But as Baker's book and other histories go on to explain, the New Orleans political culture was not as yielding or flexible as the city's freewheeling character might indicate and changes came with great difficulty. As Robert Crain, in *The Politics of School Desegregation*, summarizes the conflict: "It was one of the nation's most chaotic and violent school desegregations. All this, not in some landlocked Bible-belt country town, but in the nation's second largest port, home of liberal French Catholicism, and one of America's most cosmopolitan cities, thronged with tourists and business men from all over the world—cultured, civilized, heterogenous New Orleans."[19]

Under court order to desegregate the schools, but fearing public outcry, the Orleans Parish School Board turned to Governor Jimmie Davis for aid in 1960. Davis, who had vowed to prevent any African American student from ever attending school with a white child, issued an executive order in which he assumed control of the Orleans Parish schools. The legislature backed him with a slew of anti-integration laws. Seeing things differently, the court nullified the action of the state and once again ordered the board to comply. The board permitted the transfer of five African American girls and sent them to two schools in the Ninth Ward. Although desegregation would have surely encountered difficulty anywhere, the board's selection of the Ninth Ward effectively condemned the city to intense and violent opposition. The schools' location in the same neighborhood allowed desegregation opponents to more easily focus their efforts in one area. Furthermore, the ward bordered Leander Perez country, with one of the schools only a few blocks from the Plaquemines Parish line. More important, the Ninth Ward was inhabited by working-class whites living in projects and repeatedly neglected by the city's elite. It had been the last area of New Orleans to receive street lights and paved roads. Robert Crain describes the community's reaction to this disparity:

> Politically, socially, and economically, the city has been dominated by the Anglo-Americans, who live uptown ("above"—west of—Canal Street), and the Creole French, who live in the French Quarter. In the nineteenth century the area east of the French Quarter was the immigrant truck-gardening section of the city, composed of Germans, Italians, and non-Creole French. Though many of these people have achieved middle class status, their section of town is still politically weak. Suddenly they discovered that two of their schools—and none in any other section of town—had been desegregated. To the residents of the ninth ward the decision seemed motivated by pure malice, and even upper-middle-class moderates were furious.[20]

To many of these whites, desegregation would deny them the one token that bolstered their sense of social worth:

> Many of them had been defeated in the competition for material success and were least equipped psychologically to handle the added humiliation they believed racial desegregation of their children's schools would impose. That they lived in a housing project already had de-

moted them to the level of the black families who lived in the nearby all-black project. "At least I'm not a nigger" counted for less now than it once had. The prospect of black children transferring from the neighborhood black schools to the neighborhood white schools promised the final injustice.[21]

Soon whites were boycotting the schools and picketing. One sign read, "If you are poor, mix; if you are rich, forget about it; some law!"[22]

The state tried to enter the fray again. Davis called several special legislative sessions and passed many stiff anti-integration laws. Among other things, these abolished the Orleans Parish School Board, forbade all transfers, ordered the closing of any school under a desegregation order, and revoked the accreditation of integrated schools and the certification of any teachers at those schools. By November of 1960 the state legislature had assumed direct oversight of the Orleans Parish schools. The court again blocked state action. Judge J. Skelly Wright issued restraining orders against every state legislator, making Louisiana the first state to have its entire legislature enjoined. The restraining orders were issued at the request of the Orleans Parish School Board, the same board that had pled for state intervention only five months earlier.[23]

Meanwhile, violence erupted on the streets of New Orleans. Outspoken segregationists arrived on the scene to push their cause. Leander Perez goaded the crowd at a rally in the city: "Don't wait for your daughters to be raped by these Congolese. Don't wait until the burr-heads are forced into your schools. Do something about it now!"[24] Indeed, they did not wait. White mobs throwing stones and bottles attacked African Americans. Street fights broke out between whites and blacks. The whites picketing in front of the Ninth Ward schools harassed not only blacks but also whites who refused to participate in the boycott. Two very different sources reveal the rabid violence of the time—the Louisiana State Advisory Committee's report to the U.S. Commission on Civil Rights and eminent author John Steinbeck, who visited New Orleans at the time. First, the committee report:

> During the last days of November, Reverend Lloyd Foreman and Mrs. James Gabrielle, who had continued to take their children to the Frantz school, were subjected to abuse and physical violence by the mob in front of the school. This, coupled with the fact that several par-

ents in the Frantz school area had appealed to S.O.S. [Save Our Schools] for help in returning their children to school, led to the organization of a volunteer "carlift," run by parents from the uptown section of New Orleans, which transported the children to school in relative safety. The "carlift" began on December 1. The car carrying Yolanda Gabrielle was stoned and manhandled by the mob. Later in the week, it was pursued for two miles by a truck which had tried to ram it. Until Wednesday, December 7, the drivers and the women who escorted the children into the school were subjected to the vilest sort of shouted abuse from the daily-assembled crowds. . . .

The parents were subjected to an organized telephone campaign of threats and abuse. Their homes and other properties were stoned, as was one of the mothers of a child at Frantz. The jobs of the fathers were threatened; four of them lost their jobs. . . . The volunteer drivers were threatened with death, arson, disfigurement . . . in a concerted telephone campaign. . . . With the exception of a couple of juveniles alleged to have stoned Mrs. Marion McKinley [mother of white children at Frantz], no one connected with the demonstrations was arrested, nor was the mob in front of the school dispersed or told to move on.[25]

John Steinbeck paints an even more vivid picture:

The crowd was waiting for the white man who dared to bring his white child to school [Rev. Lloyd Foreman]. And here he came along the guarded walk . . . leading his frightened child by the hand. . . . The muscles of his cheeks stood out from clenched jaws, a man afraid who by his will held his fears in check. . . . A shrill, grating voice rang out. The yelling was not in chorus. . . . The crowd broke into howls and roars and whistles of applause. This is what they had come to see and hear.

No newspaper had printed the words these women shouted. It was indicated that they were indelicate, some even said obscene. On television the sound track was made to blur or had crowd noises cut in to cover. But now I heard the words, bestial and filthy and degenerate.

The words written down are dirty, carefully and selectedly filthy. But there was something far worse here than the dirt, a kind of frightening witches' Sabbath. Here was no spontaneous cry of anger, of in-

> sane rage . . . no principle good or bad. . . . The crowd behind the barrier roared and cheered and pounded one another with joy.[26]

The boycott continued for months as people across the country watched the screaming, cursing, and spitting protesters on their televisions. The situation nearly threatened the 1961 Mardi Gras festivities. Under pressure from leaders in the black community, Zulu proposed canceling their parade, much to the chagrin of the mayor, who wanted to ensure the usual healthy annual infusion of tourist dollars. Once again, struggles in New Orleans society produced accompanying struggles in Mardi Gras itself. The two seem inextricable.

As a new, more modern type of parade emerged, the battle continued. The founding of Endymion in 1967 and Bacchus in 1968, immediately on the heels of the passage of landmark civil rights legislation, created the first of what would later be called "superkrewes." These were Mardi Gras krewes founded not by elitist social clubs but by new-money interests within the city who wanted to bring in tourism and attention to a region with a struggling economy. The public gravitated to these new parades, which rolled more floats and dispensed more Mardi Gras doubloons and beads than the old-line krewes of Comus, Momus, and Proteus.

The impact of the superkrewes on the festivities coincided with the beginning of an economic shift in New Orleans. Old-money interests were being displaced by the new and powerful oil and tourism industries. The construction of corporate high-rises, five-star hotels, and the Superdome in downtown New Orleans showed a city in transition. The shift brought with it a new, rising middle class and an influx of young businessmen—and businesswomen—from above the Mason-Dixon line and from Texas. The days of political and social domination by the city's old elite were numbered.

A city council meeting in late 1991 became the battleground between those wanting to integrate Mardi Gras parades and krewes and the city's elite, which had controlled the celebration for over a century. Led by Councilwoman Dorothy Mae Taylor, the New Orleans council was now majority black and was threatening to withhold the most coveted of city gifts, parade permits, from any Mardi Gras krewe that could not prove it did not discriminate. At issue was not only Mardi Gras parades but also the image of New Orleans as a whole. Since the economic shift from the oil boom of the 1970s to a city comfortable with its huge tourist industry, local leaders had become more in tune with the demands of being racially progressive and politically tolerant. They understood that to retain huge conventions, sporting events, and Carnival tourists, the city could not be seen as an Old South, segregationist aristocracy.

Many issues were involved with the ordinance at hand. The krewes argued that they were private organizations and as such were allowed to pick and choose whomever they wanted for their organization. Taylor and her supporters responded by saying that the krewes were not entitled to call themselves private organizations when one of their biggest functions involved parading on city streets, being escorted by city police, and being cleaned up after by city sanitation workers. The krewes countered that the Carnival season, of which they were an important if not vital part, brought a $500 million impact to the local economy, the only substitute for the lack of new business in the city. They further claimed that their own philanthropic gifts to the city, including one krewe member's management of City Park for one dollar a year, were worth more than the city's subsidization of their parades. However, Taylor fired back by repeatedly showing the krewes as secretive and discriminatory, asking pointed questions about their secret practices and their all-white membership rolls. As numerous citizens came forward to testify before the council, it became clear that things were not going the way the krewes expected.

The krewe leaders decided to compromise. The ordinance regarding parade permits would be adopted, but a year-long investigation by a "blue ribbon committee on Carnival" would be granted before any real action was taken. The council would then vote on any recommendations by the committee. Despite the year-long moratorium, the effects of the decision were virtually immediate.

Momus, one of the oldest Mardi Gras krewes, canceled its parade for the 1992 season. Comus, the oldest, followed. Despite the absence of these two classic krewes from the streets, most remember the Carnival season of 1992 as very typical of Mardi Gras past. The age of the old-line dominance of Mardi Gras had passed.

Nevertheless, the "blue ribbon committee," with a ratio of two whites to one black in its membership, became a thorn in the side of those hoping to desegregate Mardi Gras krewes. The committee presented the city council with several recommendations that in effect watered down the original ordinance. Among those recommendations was an amendment that required krewes to sign a written affidavit stating that they had no discriminatory policies. In essence, if a krewe was accused of discriminating, they needed only to deny it in order to be found innocent.

The recommendations passed, but they were insufficient for some traditionalists. Joining Comus and Momus, the old-line krewe of Proteus pledged not to parade again. Perhaps its members feared prosecution for perjury if they signed the required affidavit; apparently they gave little consideration to the expedient of simply integrating the krewe. Proteus' decision not to parade in 1993 virtually brought an end to old-line Mardi Gras. The wooden carriages that had carried the kings of Carnival for over a century were now replaced by the fiberglass flotillas of the superkrewes. Although a later court decision allowed for the private association of the Boston, Pickwick, and Louisiana Clubs, all somehow tied in with old-line Carnival krewes, and basically stated they could openly discriminate, the krewes failed to parade again.

The history of Mardi Gras and of New Orleans shows the complex connection between festival and city politics. The evolution of one was clearly and mutually the evolution of the other, and as the economy and politics of a city changed, so did the leadership and makeup of Carnival. As Calvin Trillin wrote in an insightful 1998 article in *The New Yorker* titled "New Orleans Unmasked": "Decades after the grip of the clubmen on the city's economy loosened—and decades, for that matter, after the old-line parades were what the *profanum vulgus* found most exciting about Carnival—it stands to reason that the old-money krewes would retreat to exercising their good taste among their own."[27]

On the one hand, the Louisiana political culture of heavy-handed elite competition helped New Orleans maintain its Old World charm and allowed it to retain its rightful place as one of this country's most interesting cities. On the other hand, this created an aristocratic culture that led to huge social and economic inequalities. After the civil rights movement, as the older aristocracy lost some of its power and city opened itself up to outsiders, tourism became the most significant economic engine.

While the social progress of the city is unquestionably worthwhile, the nostalgia for the old culture remains among even the most progressive observers of the city. In 1987, New Orleans–born journalist and author Nicholas Lemann wrote a piece for *Harper's* magazine that makes the yearning for the old almost palpable:

> As late as the sixties the charms of New Orleans were mostly unself-conscious by-products of local history and ethnicity. Now they're becoming the province of marketers going after the convention trade. The locus of traditional jazz has moved from nightclubs to hotels. Festivals (like the new French Quarter Festival) arise not from traditional motives but from the perception that there is a gap to fill in the round of tourist festivities. There is talk of a new streetcar line along the river [now complete], not to take people to work but to fulfill tourists' assumption that New Orleans means streetcars. When I was a reporter at an underground newspaper in the French Quarter, during the early seventies, the staffers used to have coffee and beignets (which we called doughnuts, a word that's since been banned because it's not colorful enough) at the Morning Call, and red beans and rice at Buster Holmes, both ageless, fabulously seedy establishments whose clienteles ranged effortlessly from heroin addicts to debutantes. Now the Morning Call has moved to Fat City, and Buster Holmes to the "food court" at the Jax Brewery.[28]

The elite culture no longer dominates. As Edward Haas concluded in his study "Historical Continuity in the Crescent City," for the journal *Louisiana History:* "Although family and tradition have remained vitally important on the New Orleans scene, more and more business leaders in the Crescent City are 'not from here,' to use the vernacular."[29] New Orleans, like Louisiana, may be losing its distinctiveness. However, it is just as likely the city is experiencing another changing of the elite guard.

Why Aren't Baton Rouge Mayors from Baton Rouge?

East Baton Rouge Parish sits on the Mississippi River where south Louisiana begins to fade into the northern region and where Interstate 10 brings the western and eastern portions of the state together. The parish seat, Baton Rouge, also serves as the state capital. In most of the twentieth century, the city was anchored economically by the two major state universities, the state government, and the Exxon oil refinery. They provided a constant source of blue-collar and service employment, and local politics reflected that demographic. These state, city, and oil-refinery employees tended to vote as labor-oriented Democrats. In the 1970s, due mainly to the economic surge provided by increased oil prices, the population of the city grew rapidly and changed demographically. Baton Rouge, and especially southeast Baton Rouge, experienced almost frenetic suburbanization. In fact, one suburban Baton Rouge zip code, 70815, had the largest population growth in the state in the decade of the seventies. The population boom brought with it a change in politics, as the surburbanites tended to have white-collar jobs and to vote Republican.

Despite the fact that thousands of self-described Baton Rouge residents have exploded beyond the city's limits to swallow a large part of the parish, East Baton Rouge Parish is also home to two smaller incorporated cities, Baker and Zachary. Until the middle of the twentieth century, Baton Rouge and these other towns were governed by their own municipal leaders while the parish was led by a separate police jury.

In 1948 Baton Rouge passed a government reorganization plan that consolidated, but did not combine, city and parish government. The city council remained intact, but its powers were limited. The new parish council consisted of members of the city council and elected representatives from areas of the parish outside the city limits. Its proponents viewed the new form of government as an innovative, sensible approach to city/county management. It was certainly sold as such to the voters. The *Baton Rouge Morning Advocate*'s August 5, 1947, editorial urging voters to support the new charter concluded by asserting that "Baton Rouge and East Baton Rouge Parish will line up with these forward-looking communities in adopting for itself a modern and more efficient form of government."[30]

Although the new system may have been innovative in terms of institutional restructuring, it eventually led to some awkward city politics. It was clear that, intentionally or not, the new form of government provided another way for the ruling elite in the city to consolidate its power. The less prosperous inner city seemed most destined to suffer politically.

This combined city-parish council was headed by a mayor-president, who was both mayor of the city of Baton Rouge and president of the parish council. Because of the latter job, the mayor of Baton Rouge did not have to be a resident of the city. Indeed, serving office in a smaller municipality of the parish has become a springboard for election to the Baton Rouge mayor's office. For the sixteen years from 1964 to 1980, non-city resident W. W. "Woody" Dumas served as the mayor of Baton Rouge. From 1988 to 2000, the former mayor of Zachary, Tom Ed McHugh, served as Baton

Rouge's top official. In 2000 East Baton Rouge Parish elected a former Baker mayor, Bobby Simpson, over Baton Rouge resident and state representative Kip Holden. Ironically, the one Baton Rouge resident who was elected Baton Rouge mayor-president in the last forty years, Pat Screen, was a New Orleans native who became well known in the capital city because of his stint as quarterback of the LSU football team.

During Screen's term the population of the entire parish had grown very quickly, with the population growth outside the city limits disproportionately white. The population within the city limits of Baton Rouge had grown as well and had become disproportionately African American. Therefore the city council's racial proportions became increasingly African American, while the parish council's had not. The parish government was reorganized. The city council was dissolved and a single Metropolitan Council for both city and parish was created from the former parish council in 1982. A still-pending lawsuit charges that the change was made to dilute African American representation. Innovative? Yes. Political? You bet.

"Just a Suburb of Dallas"

The attitude toward Shreveport from the more populous, prosperous southern part of the state, especially New Orleans, was summed up fairly well by New Orleans state senator Hank Braden when he laughingly said, "I mean, Shreveport is a suburb of Dallas!"[31] But in the beginning of the twenty-first century Shreveport is proving to be the politically and economically dynamic urban heart of north Louisiana .

In the 1960s, Shreveport was also the largest city in the nation to try the experimental commission form of government. Was it reform or just politics? As in Baton Rouge, the evolution of that form points to the latter.

The form of city government that Shreveport adopted was invented in Galveston, Texas, at the beginning of the twentieth century. Even though neither Galveston nor any other Texas municipality uses this form of government anymore, Texans are characteristically boastful of its invention—even referring to it as the "Galveston Plan." A Texas government publication explains how it works:

> The commission form of city government, also known as the Galveston Plan, was devised in Galveston in 1901 and became one of

the three basic forms of municipal government in the United States. (The others are mayor-council and council-manager.) Under the commission plan voters elect a small governing commission, typically five or seven members, on an at-large basis. As a group the commissioners constitute the legislative body of the city responsible for taxation, appropriations, ordinances, and other general functions. Individually, each commissioner is in charge of a specific aspect of municipal affairs, e.g., public works, finance, or public safety. One of the commissioners is designated chairman or mayor, but his function is principally one of presiding at meetings and serving in ceremonial capacities. Thus the commission plan blends legislative and executive functions in the same body.[32]

Blended government means effective and efficient government. The logic for the commission form of government was that the city should be run like a business, with each commissioner overseeing a particular area of its functions. Moreover, since there was no city council with representatives from all over the city, supposedly there would be less "politics" involved in the business of governing. But politics out means politics in. As it turned out, installation of the new system allowed the established elite in Shreveport to control the government more than ever. Since all commissioners were elected at-large and no one was elected from smaller districts covering each section of the city, only politicians who had the considerable resources to win citywide could serve in city government. And, of course, for all the high-sounding rhetoric about removing "politics" from the process, the dirty little secret was that commissions did make political decisions (prioritizing projects, deciding what parts of the city to spend resources on), and the commission form allowed a few already powerful people to control these decisions without input from citizens throughout Shreveport. Innovative? Absolutely. Political? You bet.

Eventually, with the passage of the Voting Rights Act in 1965 and similar legislation, the commission form seemed destined to be replaced. According to former mayor John Hussey, however, it was probably the allegations surrounding Shreveport public safety commissioner George D'Artois and his possible connections with the murder of advertising executive Jim Leslie that gave the move to change the last bit of momentum it needed.[33] In fact Hussey said that by the time the vote to replace the commission form of government was at hand, the debate was more about which form of government would replace it.[34]

Once the commission was replaced by a mayor-council government in 1978, previously weak groups like suburbanites and African Americans gained a much larger say in city governance. The complete changing of the guard came in 1990 when the city, previously dominated by a succession of established white Democratic men, witnessed a mayoral runoff between Hazel Beard, a white Republican woman, and C. O. Simpkins, a black Democratic icon of the civil rights movement. Beard won the election with 38,683 votes to 26,367 votes for Simpkins.

Today, politics is changing once again in Shreveport with popular mayor Keith Hightower governing with a black-white Democratic coalition that mimics political evolution as seen in Dallas or Nashville. Statewide, people are trying to build similar coalitions, said Lanny Keller, whose position as former editorial writer for the *Shreveport Journal* and now for the *Baton Rouge Advocate* gives him valuable comparative insight into the two cities. He observed that, while Shreveport is often seen as separate from the rest of Louisiana, the nature of the city's politics is so deeply Louisianian that Shreveport often serves as the best precursor of statewide trends. If Keller is right, Louisiana may be on the verge of more racial-coalition politics.[35]

Summing Up: Power Politics in the Parishes and the Cities

In 1986, Margaret Thatcher, the Conservative prime minister of Great Britain, grew weary of the steady barrage of snipes she saw on placards across the street from the Parliament at the home of the Labour Party–leaning government of the City of London. She did something many Louisianians could understand: she pushed through legislation to abolish the government of the City of London and then she sold the building to a private enterprise.

Louisiana statewide politicians build power through direct relationships with the "courthouse gangs" in the parishes and the cities. There are several instances of blunt intervention by the state in local politics. Earl Long's actions toward New Orleans and the attempts by the legislature under Jimmie Davis to take over the Orleans Parish School system are not the only notorious examples of a governor and legislature wielding power against local authorities for political gain. In 1935 Governor O. K. Allen intervened in the statewide election by sending the National Guard into New Orleans to seize the office of the voter registrar and see to it that Long's candidates were elected.[36]

While power usually flows from the state to the local governments, there have been some notable instances where the relationship was a distinctly two-way street. Probably the most illustrative example is Leander Perez using his power as district attorney of Plaquemines Parish during the height of the desegregation conflicts to raise his status in state government as one of the most powerful opponents of integration. Lawrence Chehardy of Jefferson Parish and several other parish assessors have made it almost impossible for state politicians to touch the sacred homestead exemption. While the state almost completely controls local politics, these are among several instances where the locals can and do have an effect on state politics.

Often, as seen in twentieth-century cases of structural changes in Shreveport and Baton Rouge, city politics reflects the state political culture. Both cases provide clear instances of groups building a coalition and consolidating their wins through changing the rules of governing. These city officials obviously learned their politics in a state where rules are not sacred, because there is no common culture.

In New Orleans, the Louisiana culture is reflected even in its world-class festival of Carnival and Mardi Gras. It is fitting that the best insight into the workings of Louisiana's largest city is often obtained by discovering who's throwing the plastic beads to whom.

5. Change

A Long Way from Foster to Foster

It's almost eerie. Louisiana ended the nineteenth century with Murphy James Foster serving as governor and ended the twentieth century with his grandson Murphy James Foster Jr. in the same office. In the hundred years between them, three governors, known in Louisiana simply as "Huey," "Earl," and "Edwin," dominated the political landscape. Not surprisingly, two of those were brothers. Throughout a century of cries for political reform and even revolution, Louisiana politics could not even manage a name change.

Yet at the beginning of the twenty-first century, there are some very real indications that Louisiana has changed profoundly. The monumental political and social changes brought by the civil rights movement and women's rights movement were the most spectacular aspects of the evolution of the Louisiana culture in the twentieth century. In addition, Louisiana's French-speaking residents were subject first to the suppression of their language and culture in the beginning of the century and then to a celebration of both toward the end of the century.

The discovery of oil at the very start of the century had an enormous impact on the health and makeup of the economy. The eventual fall of oil prices was almost equally consequential. The power of the governor declined, racial voting increased, public policy toward education changed, and the power of business interests grew. Finally, the amount of political corruption may also be on the decline.

There is also equally real and convincing evidence—Foster to Foster, Long to Long—that nothing has changed at all. Louisiana politics remains volatile and competitive, and the state continues at the bottom of most lists of indicators of good state characteristics and the top of most lists of bad characteristics (see table 5-A, Appendix 2). In typical Louisiana fashion, paradox is the rule, and both continuity and change in Louisiana are true.

Civil Rights Changing Everything and Nothing

A straightforward argument can easily be made that, despite all of the clever and cute name coincidences, Louisiana in 2000 differed so fundamentally from Louisiana in 1900 that there is absolutely no basis for continuity in political culture. Even the latter-day Governor Foster (who, unlike his grandfather, calls himself "Mike") rejects what might be an appealing opportunity to make connections. When a sixth-grader at Elm Grove Middle School in Bossier Parish asked Governor Foster in a letter for a Black History Month assignment about Foster's grandfather's support of segregation, Foster responded that his grandfather "was a good, honest, decent man. . . . Of course, no one in modern times is in favor of segregation. I am sure if he lived now he would not be in favor of it, either."[1]

The dramatic unfolding of the civil rights movement was the most obvious major change in Louisiana politics in the century. After all, until that movement's success, roughly one-third of the Louisiana population was not able to participate fully—or, in most cases, at all—in the political process. The emergence of African Americans as a forceful presence in the politics of Louisiana served to further destabilize the already tenuous balance of the political culture.

To be sure, black battles and victories in Louisiana have been impressive. Several key brave struggles early in the civil rights movement occurred in Louisiana. Adam Fairclough, who thoroughly documented these events in his book *Race and Democracy: The Civil Rights Struggle in Louisiana*, argues that it was the early racial fight *in Louisiana* that "provided the strong base, the bedrock, of the civil rights movement."[2] A Baton Rouge bus boycott in 1953 set the stage for the Montgomery bus boycott two years later that began with Rosa Parks defying the law and defined the movement for years to follow. Ralph Abernathy and Martin Luther King were key leaders of the Montgomery boycott. In his autobiography, Abernathy credits the Baton Rouge boycott for providing "considerable inspiration."[3] For the organizational planning of the Montgomery boycott, King consulted the leader and spokesman of the Baton Rouge action, Reverend T. J. Jemison, King's college roommate and longtime friend.[4]

Another early and sometimes violent Louisiana front in the civil rights wars was Bogalusa. A paper-mill town east almost to the Mississippi state line, Bogalusa was one of the few places in the United States where the Ku Klux Klan met with forceful, organized black resistance. The Bogalusa struggles are the subject of an acclaimed book by Peter Jan Honigsberg, *Crossing Border Street: A Civil Rights Memoir.*[5]

Although, as Fairclough is quick to note, complete racial equality remains elusive, there have been measurable gains. Despite the fact that Louisiana has yet to elect an African American to any statewide office—and that only rarely has an African American won any elective office where blacks are in a minority—the state has seen a rise in African American voting and substantial increases in the number of black elected officials: the statewide tally exploded from a mere 33 in 1968 to 333 in 1978 and has grown steadily since that time.[6] In 1967 former New Orleans mayor Ernest "Dutch" Morial became the first black elected to the state legislature since Reconstruction. Today 22 African Americans are among the 105 members of the Louisiana House of Representatives and 9 of the 39 members of the Louisiana Senate are African American.

Given all of these gains, the civil rights movement clearly transformed the substance of Louisiana politics. Yet it played only a reinforcing role in the Louisiana *style* of politics. After all, as one of the three well-defined groups gains a larger voice and is on more of an equal footing with the other two, conflict among all three groups may even heighten. In the latter third of the twentieth century, African Americans joined northern European Americans and southern European Americans as the three distinct, well-defined pillars of the Louisiana politics of competition and heterogeneity.

The battle for political rights of women in Louisiana was also hard-fought. Although the two social movements were different in form and in kind, they exhibit a similar pattern. Gains have been pronounced, yet complete equality remains elusive. The first woman in the Louisiana legislature was Doris Lindsey Holland, elected to the state senate in 1936. Even today Louisiana has one of the lowest proportions of women legislators in the United States, with only three in the senate and twenty in the house of representatives.

Other gains are more notable. Louisiana elected a woman to the United States Senate in 1996, two women have served as state treasurer, in 1999 a woman won the office of commissioner of elections, and women were elected lieutenant governor in both 1991 and 1995. Finally, in 2003,

Kathleen Blanco was elected governor.

In sum, while Louisiana of 1900 and Louisiana of 2000 were a century of progress apart for African Americans and for women, that century did not change Louisiana's underlying culture. After all the gains, the political importance of the ethnic diversity of Louisiana is greater now than ever.

As American as Crawfish Pie?

On the other hand, the ethnic group that symbolizes Louisiana distinctiveness may be on the decline. All ethnic cultures in America have been the subject of homogenization, and southern European culture in Louisiana is no exception. Sociologists have developed a cottage industry of writing books on ethnic blending and assimilation into a single American culture. The titles of books and articles on the subject often use terms like *Americanization*—or even *McDonaldization*—to describe the sublimation of unique ethnic groups into one dominant culture.

The Cajun culture, as Louisiana's predominantly French southern European culture is universally known, has become part of that assimilation. In an almost over-the-top homage to boudin, the Cajun dish of rice dressing stuffed in sausage casing, Calvin Trillin pithily sums up Americanized Cajun cuisine when he laments that "the word 'Cajun' on a menu is simply a synonym for burnt fish or too much pepper." Trillin elaborates: "When I am daydreaming of boudin, it sometimes occurs to me that all the indignities the Acadians of Louisiana have had visited upon them—being booted out of Nova Scotia, being ridiculed as rubes and swamp rats by neighboring Anglophones for a couple of centuries, being punished for speaking their own language in the schoolyard—nothing has been as deeply insulting as what restaurants outside South Louisiana present as Cajun food."[7]

He is right. Americanization of the French culture is an issue taken very seriously in south Louisiana. In fact, in 1968 the Louisiana legislature created the Council for the Development of French in Louisiana (or CODOFIL, as it is commonly known) to "do any and all things necessary to accomplish the development, utilization, and preservation of the French language as found in Louisiana for the cultural, economic and touristic benefit of the state."[8]

Because of this high consciousness of things Cajun, the results of the 2000 United States Census created quite a stir in south Louisiana. The census indicated that the proportion of Louisiana residents who said that they were of "some sort of French descent" had dropped from 25 percent of the population in 1990 to 16 percent in 2000. There is disagreement over both the validity of the numbers and their implications for the health of the Cajun culture. The issue of validity centers on whether the Census Bureau phrased its questions in a way that produced an underestimate of the number of residents with French descent. Barry Ancelet, a professor of Francophone studies at the University of Louisiana at Lafayette, in a recent newspaper article explains the problem: "Among the choices of French and French Canadian, the latter dropped by far the most, from 519,118 in 1990 to 179,739. Cajun was not offered as a choice, but those who wrote it in were grouped with French Canadian."[9] He goes on to argue that other wording changes, including the use of lumping French in with "other Indo-European languages" in some census forms, may have skewed the results.[10] (Given this controversy, the maps in chapter 1 of this book are based on 1990 census figures.)

The number of Louisiana residents who claim French heritage is a significant issue locally, but the sense of ethnic consciousness is important as well. CODOFIL has made meaningful strides in promoting the French culture and language. Louisiana prohibited teaching French in public schools for almost fifty years, from 1921 until 1968 (although, especially in later years, the law was not strictly enforced). In the 1960s, official attitudes changed dramatically. In 1968, not only was legislation passed to allow French language in schools, the CODOFIL bill was intended specifically to promote it. The policy seems to be working at least to some degree, but the battle to save the ethnic heritage is not easy. As David Cheramie, past director of CODOFIL, puts it, "It's true that assimilation is continuing, but I think we've slowed it down a lot."[11]

Is the distinctive southern European culture alive and well? A drive down Louisiana Highway 1 along Bayou Lafourche south of Baton Rouge yields mixed results. Sandwiched between the signs promoting boudin and Cajun dancing are McDonald's and other staples of Americana. The number of French-heritage Louisiana residents is likely to be waning at least a little. However, for now, the nature of the trend in southern European culture in south Louisiana appears to be somewhere between a small resurgence and a pugnacious slow decline.

Oil Fueling the Culture

The story of the other pillar of Louisiana uniqueness, the oil-and-gas-dominated economy, is a totally different matter. The evidence here is unmistakable and incontrovertible . In 1900, Louisiana had not yet experienced the oil and gas discovery that would revolutionize the state economy. By 2000, Louisiana was no longer an oil-economy-dominated state. The rise and eventual fall of the dominance of the oil economy had a very different effect on the culture than the strengthening effect of the civil rights movement or the determined perseverance of the slowly weakening southern European culture.

It was in the summer of 1901, when oil was discovered near Jennings, that the state began a radical transformation. Before that, the effect of big money on politics and the political culture was most obvious in the great Louisiana Lottery scandals at the end of the nineteenth century. The Louisiana Lottery was a huge money-maker, subject of countless accusations of criminal activity that focused on the New York syndicate that ran and profited enormously from it. It eventually faded from existence after Congress passed a law that disallowed moving lottery tickets across state lines. After its demise, national notoriety accompanied revelations of criminal gains. It was the lottery, not oil and gas, that established the Louisiana reputation for colorful and, yes, corrupt, politics.

The eruption of oil and gas onto center stage in Louisiana politics allowed the state's unstable, multiethnic political culture to flourish. Huey Long's swift emergence to unprecedented power with a populist message might not have been inevitable, but the seeds of his style of politics were certainly sown in a very fertile soil. For most of the twentieth century, highly competitive politics fueled by promises of spoils made possible by oil-and-gas-related revenue defined and dominated Louisiana.

In the early 1980s, when the price of oil plummeted, Louisiana was again transformed. The money that gave enormous opportunities to all of the players in politics—whether they were the Longs, their allies, their opponents, or their successors—had ended abruptly. Most estimates show that oil-and-gas-related revenue dropped from over 40 percent of the state's budget in 1980 to less than 10 percent by the end of the century. (See table 5-B, Appendix 2, for a breakdown of contemporary sources of revenue in the post-oil-boom Louisiana economy.)

Governors Sputtering

The most logical, and perhaps the most hopeful, result of the demise of oil and gas revenue as part of the Louisiana budget is a decreased level of tolerance for political corruption. However, that impact is difficult to measure. Unfortunately, political scientists have not found a perfect instrument for measuring corruption. Perhaps only in Louisiana did it seem to be an important task.

There is abundant evidence, however, for how Louisiana's lessening dependence on oil and gas revenue affected several other parts of government and politics. The most obvious and telling specific ramification was in the court of the "king." After the oil bust, the politics and power of the office of governor were transformed fundamentally.

Beginning in 1983, three consecutive incumbent governors were unable to muster even 40 percent of the vote in their tries for reelection. In one case the incumbent failed even to secure enough primary votes to make the runoff. It was not a coincidence that directly after the dramatic drop in Louisiana's oil-and-gas-revenue flow, governors found themselves floundering politically. The tribulations of Governors Dave Treen, Edwin Edwards, and Buddy Roemer during the decade after the oil bust are instructive.

When Dave Treen was elected governor in 1979, the state was enjoying the fruits of its natural resources in unprecedented ways. The state budget was flush with money generated from oil and gas severance taxes. Like any good Republican, Treen—the first Republican governor of Louisiana since the Reconstruction era—responded by cutting taxes. Soon afterward, the price of oil began to drop and drop dramatically. The Treen administration was suddenly trying to find revenue rather than attempting to cut more. His political nemesis Edwin Edwards, who had not sought reelection in 1979 because of Louisiana's two-consecutive-terms limit, was ready and most willing to take advantage of the situation.

In 1983 the state was in an economic crisis of declining revenue and disappearing jobs. Treen ran for reelection trying to convince voters that he was the person to pull Louisiana back into economic stability. Edwards, the "good times" governor of eight years when the state was rich with revenue, was unrelenting in exploiting the collapse. Treen was crushed. He lost the election by over 160,000 votes—641,146 to 480,424.

Edwards assumed office in 1984 with all the flourish, confidence, and political prowess of his first two terms. The state of the state, however, was not at all the same. His attempts to revive the economy sputtered and then came to a complete halt when he was indicted on racketeering charges and spent much of 1985 and 1986 fighting the charges in federal court. After a mistrial and then an acquittal, he ran for reelection in 1987 promising to bring back the state's economic well-being—the only thing that had kept him from completing the task already, he said, was his political enemies' insistence on making him stand trial for most of his term. Although he ran second in a field of six credible candidates, he could muster only 28 percent of the vote and dropped out before the runoff, defeated.

Buddy Roemer assumed office in 1988 with the state still reeling from the drops in oil and gas revenue and no major fix in sight. During his administration, even though several gambling measures passed (in 2002 gambling tax revenue exceeded oil and gas tax revenue), it was not nearly enough to compensate for the losses, and the Louisiana economy at the end of Roemer's term remained shaky. His difficulties were typical of those that post-oil-bust governors have experienced. Roemer presented his entire "Roemer revolution" package of tax and regulatory reforms to the people in a single vote referendum, and it failed. He was later mocked by the legislators and the press for promoting the teachings of self-help psychologists and snapping rubber bands as therapy for the stress of governing. He ran for reelection and he could not beat even the discredited Edwin Edwards or former Ku Klux Klansman David Duke. In the third straight election after the oil bust, an incumbent governor ran for reelection and fell to a humiliating defeat.

After winning the 1991 "race from hell," as political pundits were quick to label it, Edwards's honeymoon ended quickly and most discussions about his administration swirled around whether his former allies, such as state treasurer Mary Landrieu, would run against him if he ran yet again and what he might do after his sixteen years of reign as governor and kingpin of the state. He decided not to run for reelection. So now four consecutive terms after the oil bust had ended in political failure for an incumbent governor, once a phenomenally commanding figure in Louisiana politics. In a state where the political persuasive power of the governor is legendary, times had fundamentally changed.

Granted, these governors had other problems—after all, Edwards spent most of his third term in court. However, all four governorships were marked by one consistent factor. These governors could no longer exercise their power the same way their predecessors had done for more than fifty years. Political victory could no longer mean consolidating power. Louisiana was suddenly too poor to fund the rewards.

Family Feud

The governor's office was not the only thing in politics to be affected by the oil bust. The drop in oil money was quickly followed by a drop in the exorbitant amounts of money spent on campaigns. The 1983 governor's race was indeed the "Last Hayride" as John Maginnis called it in his book about the race. Louisiana would never again top the charts in campaign spending for state races.

It was not just the amount of funding for campaigns that changed, though. The nature of the campaigns themselves changed. Louisianians needed to blame something or someone not only for falling state revenues but also for lost jobs and stagnant incomes—and politicians needed to find a way to voice their concern. That tried and true southern message of racial baiting reared its head almost on cue. Louisianians were hurting and they blamed each other.

Just like in the days of Tom Watson's harsh racial politics in Georgia at the turn of the twentieth century, poor whites responded to a politician who said the problem was that blacks were getting too much help and that black gains were by definition white losses. The voice of course was David Duke.

David Duke became a small curiosity in Louisiana politics in the early 1970s when he gave incendiary speeches on the LSU campus and founded the White Youth Alliance. One well-known photograph of him from his college days shows him picketing a speech by attorney William Kunstler at Tulane University, wearing a Nazi-style brown shirt and swastika armband and carrying a sign proclaiming, "Kunstler is a Communist-Jew." After he graduated from college, Duke became a wizard of the Ku Klux Klan and organized rallies in the rural outskirts of Baton Rouge. He tried repeatedly to begin a political career, running unsuccessfully for the state legislature in 1975 and 1979 and even for president of the United States in 1988. Finally, in 1989, he narrowly won the seat for the remainder of a term in the Louisiana House of Representatives. This gave him the political soap box he needed to become a player in state politics. William B. McMahon, a state capitol reporter for the *Baton Rouge Advocate,* summarized Duke's time in the legislature:

> During the session, he introduced eight bills and one resolution. The bills sought to raise penalties on drug offenders in public housing projects, repeal affirmative action programs, repeal minority set-aside programs, require drug testing of young, first-time applicants for driver's licenses, require drug testing for public assistance, and provide loss of entitlements for drug offenders.
>
> Debate on the bills—none passed—generally produced arguments grounded in race. On the surface Duke's presentations were couched in mainstream Republicanisms. "There is massive institutional racial discrimination going on in this state and nation now. And it's against whites," Duke told a house committee in arguing for a bill to abolish affirmative action and minority set-asides. "I believe in equal rights for everybody—special privilege for no one," Duke said. The black member of the panel, Representative Joe Delpit of Baton Rouge, responded when asked if he objected to the bill, "I'm objecting to the author." The bill was approved by the committee on a 5-1 vote, with three of the five yes votes from Republicans. Delpit voted no and walked out in protest.[12]

Having raised his statewide profile in the legislature, Duke ran in 1990 for the United States Senate. He stunned the political community by winning 44 percent of the vote statewide in his bid to defeat incumbent senator Bennett Johnston. Although Johnston won with 752,902 votes to 607,391 for Duke, any cursory analysis of parish and precinct returns would show Duke receiving a majority of the white vote—from 55 to 60 percent of it, according to publicly reported estimates. With this base, Duke was poised to run for governor in 1991.

The timing of Duke's meteoric rise to prominence was no accident. He garnered so many votes for U.S. senator and for governor because he expressed the anger caused by the downturn in the economy. He directed that anger toward programs designed to help blacks, and the message resonated.

Indeed, the only three gubernatorial runoffs since the oil bust were all marked by conspicuous racial fissures in the electorate. In 1991, Duke received almost universal hostility from black leaders and black voters in his loss to Edwards, in which Edwards tallied 1,057,031 votes to 671,009 for Duke. In 1995, Cleo Fields became the first African American to reach the runoff for governor but lost in a landslide to Mike Foster, with race being the overwhelming predictor of voter choice.[13] Then in 1999 Foster again ran against an African American candidate, William Jefferson, and the results and the vote patterns were almost identical.

With money short and no long-term relief in sight, the state's well-defined ethnic groups were not going to hold hands and work together. They were fighting for every piece of the pie. This was a contrast to the less racially polarized responses in the 1960s, when the fundamental stakes were higher but the economic foundation was stronger.

As Louisiana moves to a more diversified, and presumably more healthy, economy, such obvious and obviously destructive racial politics may begin to subside. The immediate impact of the oil bust on voting patterns, however, was to heighten racial political conflict in the state.

Earning and Learning

Although Huey Long used Louisiana's wealth to pour legendary sums into LSU, higher education was not a priority in an oil economy. During the Long era, the priorities in education were at the most basic level. Free textbooks for public schools was one of Long's rallying cries and best-known accomplishments.

His approach to higher education was distinctly populist. He wanted it to be accessible to the masses and saw to it that colleges were no more than sixty miles away from any citizen. In addition, as in most southern states, Louisiana's early segregated educational system meant that a dual white and black set of universities was created. This meant that education resources were spread very thin and that the system emphasized access rather than accomplishment.

The one place where higher education should, by definition, excel is Louisiana's flagship university, LSU. Funding for the university increased dramatically during the Long era, and over the years the university has been home to some nationally regarded departments and legendary scholars. It is no coincidence that probably the two best-known scholars associated with LSU were catapulted to scholarly superstardom because of works associated directly with Long himself.

Robert Penn Warren, the only writer ever to receive Pulitzer Prizes in both fiction and poetry, and the nation's first poet laureate, received one of those prizes for *All the King's Men* (1946), a novel widely thought to be based on the life of Huey Long. LSU historian T. Harry Williams also won a Pulitzer Prize for a book much more patently about the governor—the 1968 biography that bears his name. LSU is also noted for a history of major contributions in agricultural fields, especially sugar refinery, and of course in petroleum-related sciences and engineering.

While Long did see to it that the state invested large sums of money in its flagship university, he approached even LSU from a distinctly populist perspective. He wanted to make the successes of LSU meaningful to the common citizen who never even dreamed of attending classes. To this end, he focused much of his energy on popularizing the entertainment LSU could provide for everyone—especially the football games. He led the marching band on game days, tried to call plays for the team in Tiger Stadium, and strong-armed businesses into doing things that would support Tiger football.

As the oil and gas industry became more and more integral to the Louisiana economy through the twentieth century, the political emphasis on the academic aspect of higher education waned (although the commitment to winning football teams certainly did not). After all, a petroleum economy was an economy that provided blue-collar, well-paying jobs that did not require a college degree. A young man in the 1940s could look at an immediate healthy paycheck as a laborer in the oil fields and offshore, or he could spend four years paying for an education. As opportunities grew for employment of this kind, the economics of higher-education spending no longer made much sense.

With the oil bust in the 1980s, all of that changed. Louisiana needed to diversify its economy, and higher education—indeed, all education—became a heightened priority. After a few bumps in the road in the 1980s and 1990s, it is obvious that the legislature and the governor's office—especially under Governor Mike Foster—recognized this and began to emphasize the need for a well-funded, well-organized higher education system. Foster also tried several times to use his immense public support to overhaul the antiquated, regressive Louisiana tax structure, heavily dependent on sales taxes. He was never successful. Clearly Louisiana needed to learn in order to earn after the oil bust.

The Politics of Economic Diversification

While education was a beneficiary of the need for economic diversification, many business interests benefitted as well. Oil and gas interests provided many blue-collar jobs in Louisiana. The "Chemical Corridor" (or "Cancer Alley" as it has been christened by environmentalists) between Baton Rouge and New Orleans along the Mississippi River is lined with miles of refineries and processing plants. They provided fertile ground for organized labor groups. The AFL-CIO, under the guidance and direction of its masterful Louisiana strategist Victor Bussie, dominated the legislative lobbying scene until the late 1970s. There were earlier days of a quiet Bussie standing in the back of the legislative chamber nodding a subtle "yes" or "no" and then seeing thirty or forty votes light up in unison on the board above the podium. The power of labor in Louisiana was palpable. That has all changed.

In 1976, a few years before the oil bust, the AFL-CIO lost a critical fight to business interests with the passage of a landmark right-to-work law that permanently weakened union organizing and recruitment. In a few short years, the price of oil plummeted and the state began looking for other businesses to make up for the gap in the economy. These circumstances set the stage for one of the most fundamental political changes in Louisiana politics in the last quarter of the twentieth century. The Louisiana Association of Business and Industry, under the expert leadership of its then director, Ed Steimel, became the dominant force in the Louisiana legislature. Beginning with the landmark passage of the Louisiana Right-to-Work Law (which allows workers to refrain from joining a labor union) to holding onto the ten-year industrial property tax exemption despite strong attacks, the association has had a remarkable series of legislative successes.

In their chapter on Louisiana in a book on interest groups in the South, Charles Barrilleaux and Charles Hadley sum it up this way: "According to [lobbyist Randy] Haynie the mid-1970s witnessed the transition from legislative dominance by organized labor to that of organized business under the leadership of Steimel and LABI." They continue: "Under the banner of reform, LABI serves as the organizing force for business interests."[14]

In fact, the dominance of LABI has become so pervasive that two of its staunchest allies, including Ed Steimel himself, have been critical of its influence. In 2001, Steimel, long retired as director of the flagship business lobby, flabbergasted the journalistic community by hinting in an interview that he thought business interests had gone too far and were harming Louisiana's workers and economy at large.[15] That was followed in April 2002 by an equally startling speech by staunchly probusiness governor Mike Foster criticizing LABI for pushing its own agenda too far and not being concerned for the state as a whole. Part of the front-page account of the speech follows:

> Foster, a business owner with a long pro-business record, named no names in his speech but clearly focused his ire on LABI.
>
> "I don't know why (there is a) gulf between me and some of my friends," Foster said as he ignored his prepared speech to "get some things off my chest." Foster said he told the big-business lobby and its supporters that he would "be glad to sit down with you and work out some way" to reform taxes.
>
> The result, he said, was not a single phone call.
>
> "It worries me when I see that same organization . . . not make a single constructive idea on education, a single constructive idea on the environment, a single constructive idea in any other area, like health care," Foster told lawmakers as he opened the fiscal session.[16]

Both sets of statements were paraded across all of the state's newspapers, indicating how much the pendulum had swung from the early 1970s, when labor was the predominant interest group in Louisiana, to the early part of the twenty-first century, when business, and particularly LABI, enjoys that status and position. Once again, even the strongest grip on political power remains tentative in Louisiana.

Post Eruption, No More Corruption?

Almost every aspect of Louisiana politics was affected by the end of the oil economy. The aftershocks were profound and immediate. Louisiana could no longer afford much of anything—not even corruption.

Before the oil bust, few people in Louisiana cared about how efficiently the state spent its money. A government funded mostly by several major oil and gas companies who needed the state's resources was government as Santa Claus. People were not particularly concerned about the price of the presents, because it was not their money that was paying for them.

After the oil bust, it was. In order to fund projects and programs at previous levels, taxes would have to be raised. Logically, Louisiana citizens became more concerned about how that money was spent. Even though so little time has passed that evidence is tough to gather, the amount of corruption in Louisiana politics may naturally diminish. Louisiana can simply no longer afford its corruption. The logic is simple. During times of fat state coffers stuffed by oil companies, politicians could hire their friends in and out of government to carry out programs, build roads, construct hospitals, buy equipment, and do all the other jobs of a populist government without regard to cost efficiency. They could consolidate their power as they wastefully padded the bank accounts of their friends.

Losing the Reputation?

If, indeed, corruption begins to wane in Louisiana politics, the reputation of the state is likely to slowly evolve as well. That evolution may have already started. A few symbolic changes in state governance are leading to a limited change in perceptions of Louisiana, from the widespread image of a state whose politics is freewheeling, provincial, to one of a state closer to the national norm. Two recent articles in prestigious journals call attention to these two small but perhaps indicative developments.

The first article, in the March 14, 2002, *Economist,* is significant because Louisiana is not mentioned. It is attention by omission. It was refreshing for this Louisianian to read a description of a chaotic, almost laughable, characteristic of state government in a national magazine and realize the discussion was not about Louisiana. The article described a present state constitution as follows: "At well over 300,000 words, it is longer than *Moby Dick* and 40 times the length of the US constitution. The 1901 document itself accounts for only about a tenth of this. The rest comes from some 700 amendments, which are appearing with increasing rapidity (52 in 2000 alone)."[17] The article, about Alabama, was an indication that, although Louisiana may remain the state with the most constitutions (eleven), it no longer has the distinction of having the longest constitution with the most amendments: the 1921 Louisiana Constitution had a mere 503 amendments in 1973, when it became obsolete. This may be a small point—after all, Louisiana can still claim the second-longest state constitution in American history—but it is a small sign of normalization. Louisiana has, moreover, exhibited almost normal adherence to the present constitution, keeping it relatively intact for some thirty years.

A perhaps more symbolic change in the governance of Louisiana occurred in August 2001. Alan Ehrenhart, writing in *Governing*, the normally staid professional journal of state government, began his article on a several alterations in state bureaucracies with this striking, melodramatic proclamation: "The most ridiculous office in American state government is about to pass out of existence."[18] He was referring to the passage of legislation in the summer of 2001 that removed the office of commissioner of elections as an elective statewide office in Louisiana. Even though Ehrenhart noted later in the article that "no other state has a political culture remotely resembling Louisiana's," he nonetheless heralded the death of this one bit of Louisiana exceptionalism.

The Future

Louisiana politics in the twentieth century was a highly unstable competition among well-defined, self-conscious ethnic groups that did not trust each other. The third of the state with African American heritage did not trust the two-thirds of mostly European heritage. The Europeans in Louisiana, however, were split as well. Roughly half were of northern European origin with Protestant religious roots, and half had southern European ancestors with mainly Catholic religious ties. Since no group dominated, Louisiana politics was in constant motion. The dynamics of coalitions and conflict characterized the politics of the entire century.

The fuel for the politics was the revenue gained from the oil and gas industry, attracted by the rich natural resources in the state. The money allowed for abundant political promises, and rewards and punishments could be doled out freely to the latest winners and losers. It also allowed for a fairly provincial politics: political and social trends outside the state had less impact because they were less connected to the internecine warfare inside. And all of the monetary weaponry for political fights could be found within the borders of the state through resource severance taxes.

At the beginning of the twenty-first century, the strong tripartite ethnic identities and competition and lack of trust among them remains. They will likely dissipate somewhat as newer groups, such as Hispanics, begin to blur the ethnic lines. But large numbers of Hispanic immigrants, or any great influx of any other outsider group, is currently notable in Louisiana chiefly by its absence. Surrounding states are experiencing these demographic changes much more dramatically. Slow demographic change will calm the political waters somewhat, but until large-scale changes in the ethnic mix occur, Louisiana politics will remain constantly unsettled.

The economic fuel for this competitive culture, however, has decreased. The money to fund the government, its politics, and its private economy no longer flows primarily from big oil and gas interests. It must now be self-generated through business and individual taxes and from a more diversified economic base. Whether this new direction is defined and spearheaded by the now powerful Louisiana Association of Business and Industry or by other groups seeking to topple LABI from its perch atop the heap of Louisiana politics, only time will tell.

And while Louisiana politics will certainly remain colorful and temperamental, the new economic realities mean that much of what the government decides, and the public policies that result, will almost certainly change. These new economic realities mean that the public will not be as tolerant of the political corruption associated with making some of those policy decisions as in the past. The style of Louisiana politics will likely remain the same, but the process and substance of Louisiana government will not. Louisiana can literally no longer afford for it to be any other way.

Appendix 1: Maps

MAP 1-A: Percent Black Population by Parish

U.S. Bureau of the Census

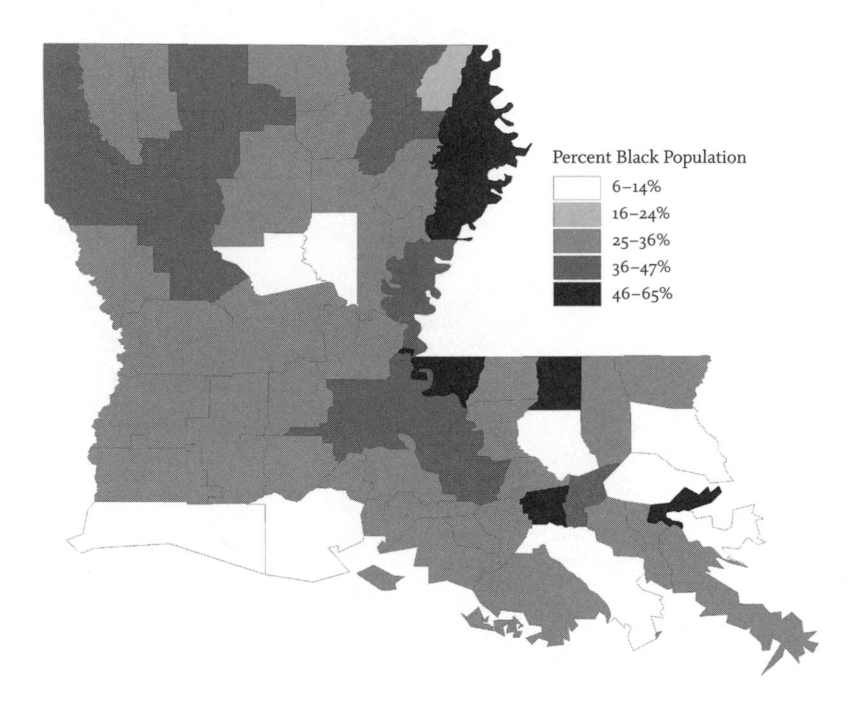

MAP 1-B: Major Religious Denominations by Parish

U.S. Bureau of the Census

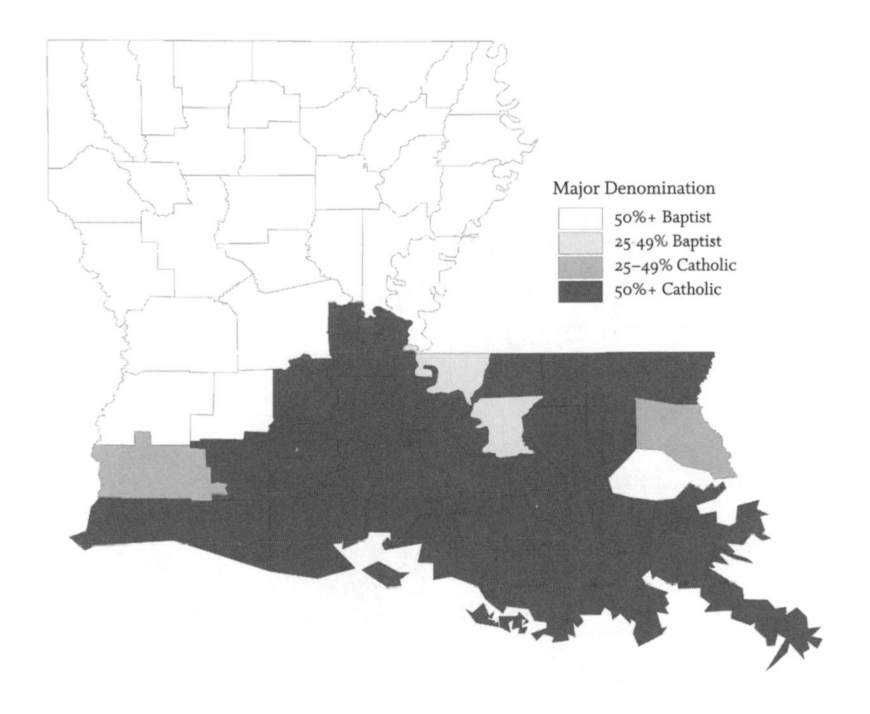

MAP 1-C: Percent French Population by Parish

U.S. Bureau of the Census

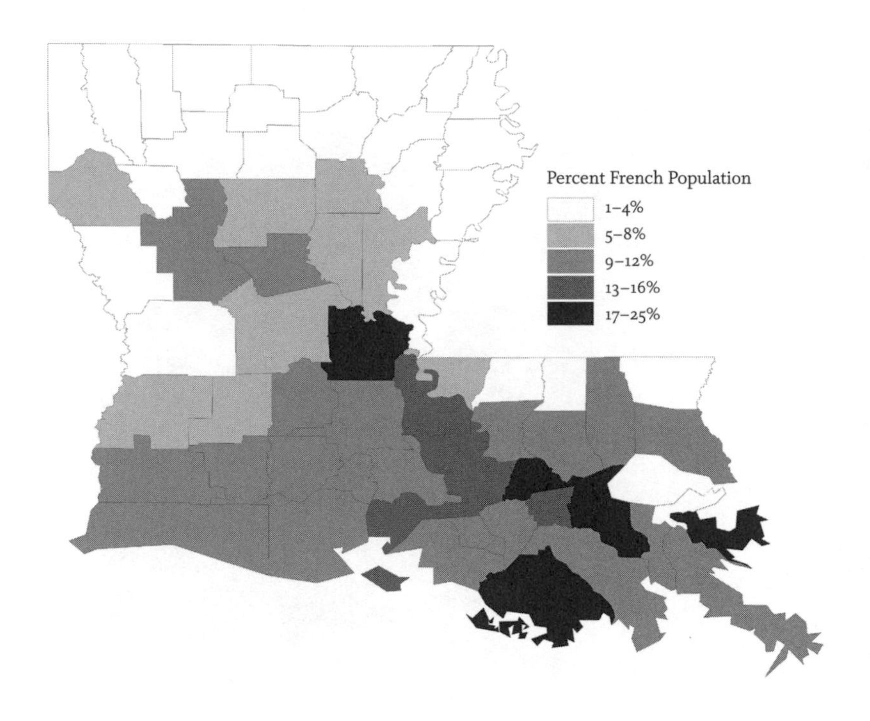

MAP 1-D: 1991 Gubernatorial Runoff by Parish

Louisiana Secretary of State

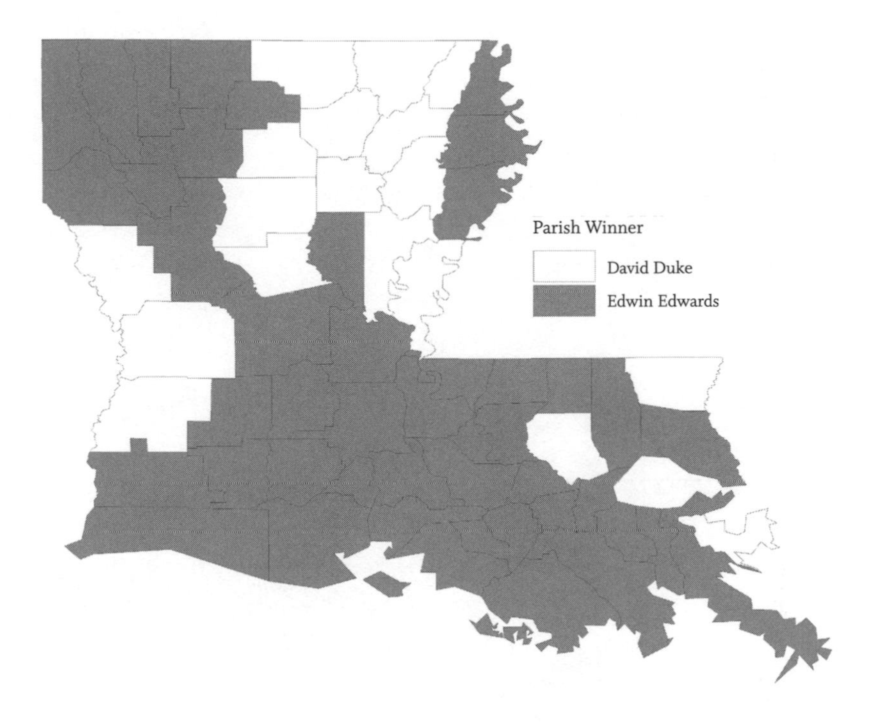

MAP 1-E: 1996 United States Senate Runoff by Parish

Louisiana Secretary of State

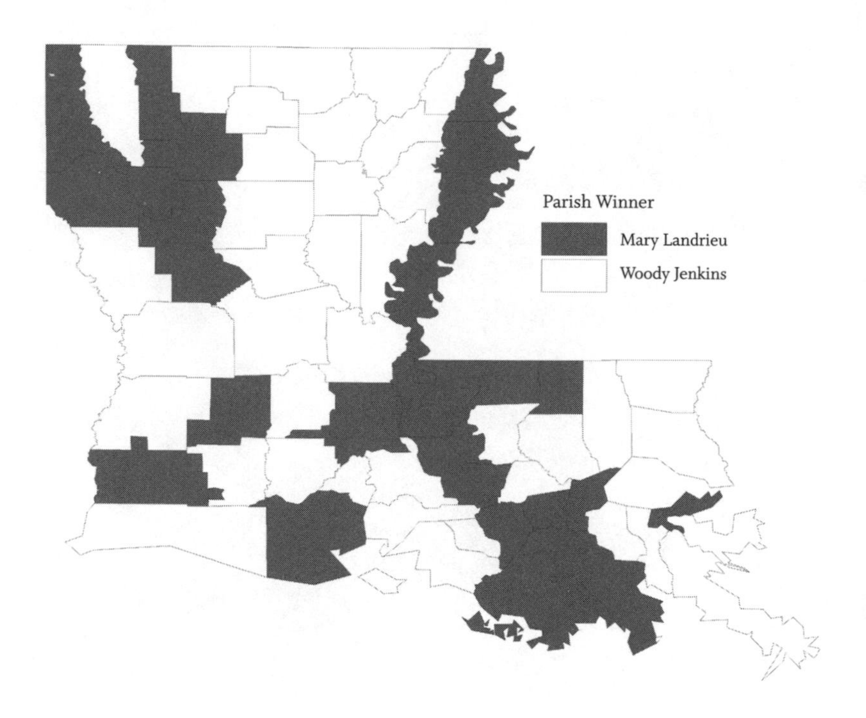

MAP 2-A: 2002 United States Senate Runoff by Parish

Louisiana Secretary of State

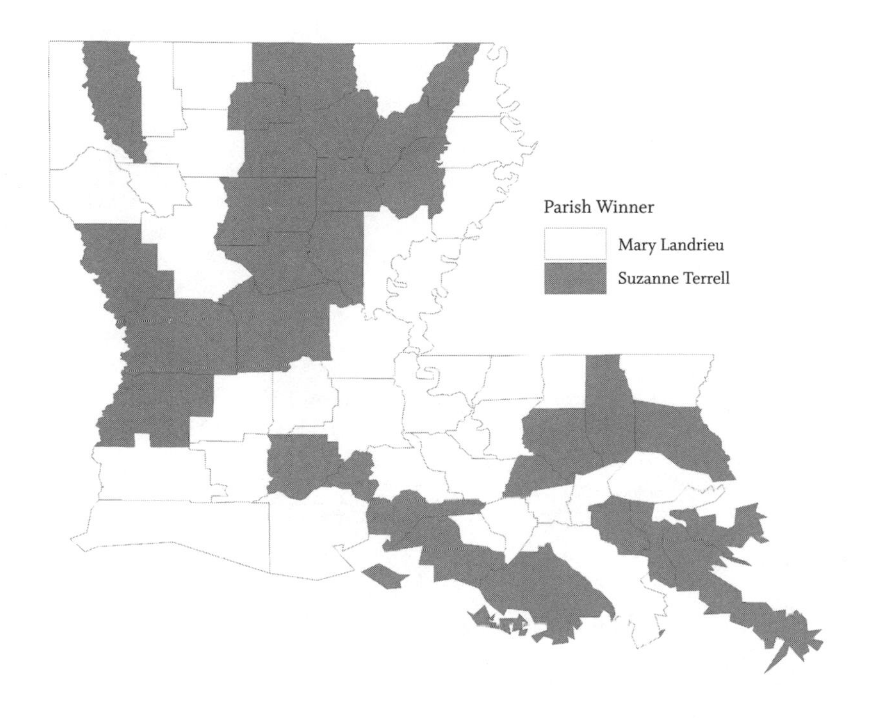

Appendix 2: Tables

TABLE 2-A

2000 Presidential Election Turnout by State *(southern states in italics)*

	State	%VAP*		State	%VAP
1.	Minnesota	68.8	26.	Pennsylvania	53.7
2.	Maine	67.4	27.	Illinois	52.8
3.	Wisconsin	66.1	28.	Utah	52.7
4.	Alaska	64.4	29.	*Virginia*	52.0
5.	Vermont	63.7	30.	Kentucky	51.7
6.	New Hampshire	62.3	31.	Maryland	51.4
7.	Montana	61.5	32.	New Jersey	51.0
8.	Iowa	60.7	33.	*Florida*	50.6
9.	Oregon	60.5	34.	*N. Carolina*	50.2
10.	North Dakota	60.4	35.	*Alabama*	50.0
11.	Wyoming	59.7	36.	New York	49.3
12.	Connecticut	58.3	37.	*Tennessee*	49.2
13.	South Dakota	58.2	38.	Indiana	49.1
14.	Missouri	57.5	39.	Oklahoma	48.8
15.	Michigan	57.4	40.	*Mississippi*	48.6
16.	Washington	56.9	41.	*Arkansas*	47.8
17.	Massachusetts	56.8	42.	New Mexico	47.4
18.	Colorado	56.8	43.	*S. Carolina*	46.5
19.	Nebraska	56.3	44.	West Virginia	45.7
20.	Delaware	56.3	45.	California	44.0
21.	Ohio	55.7	46.	*Georgia*	43.8
22.	*Louisiana*	54.2	47.	Nevada	43.8
23.	Rhode Island	54.2	48.	*Texas*	43.1
24.	Kansas	54.0	49.	Arizona	42.1
25.	Idaho	53.7	50.	Hawaii	41.0

*%VAP = Percent turnout of voting age population

SOURCE: Committee for the Study of the American Electorate, 2000: http://www.fairvote.org/turnout/preturnstate.htm.

TABLE 2-B

Average Rates of Voter Turnout in the States by Office, 1994–1997

State	Total	President	Governor	U.S. Senate	U.S. House
Montana	61.2	62.9	62.6	59.6	59.5
South Dakota	60.4	61.1	59.7	61.2	59.8
Maine	59.5	64.5	54.9	59.8	59.0
Wyoming	59.3	60.1	58.8	60.0	58.5
Minnesota	58.1	64.3	52.5	58.4	57.4
Idaho	55.6	58.2	51.5	58.8	53.8
Oregon	55.2	57.5	52.8	56.8	53.7
North Dakota	54.0	56.3	55.9	50.7	53.0
Vermont	53.8	58.6	53.6	49.3	53.6
Alaska	53.3	56.9	49.8	54.6	51.8
Iowa	53.1	57.7	46.3	57.3	51.3
New Hampshire	52.4	58.0	47.4	57.3	46.9
Nebraska	52.1	56.1	48.6	52.3	51.4
Kansas	51.4	56.6	43.5	56.1	49.3
Missouri	50.7	54.2	53.8	45.5	49.2
Massachusetts	50.5	55.3	47.4	51.6	47.7
Washington	49.7	54.7	54.3	42.5	47.5
Michigan	48.7	54.5	44.2	48.4	47.7
Connecticut	48.4	56.4	46.1	43.4	47.7
Rhode Island	48.1	52.0	47.3	46.8	46.4
Colorado	47.6	52.4	41.1	51.7	45.2
Utah	47.0	50.3	50.8	41.7	45.4
Wisconsin	46.9	57.4	41.4	41.5	47.4
Delaware	46.4	49.6	49.6	43.8	42.7
Louisiana	46.1	56.9	49.4	54.2	23.9
Ohio	45.5	54.3	40.3	41.3	46.1
Oklahoma	45.3	49.9	41.6	45.0	44.7
North Carolina	44.2	45.8	46.7	46.5	37.7
Indiana	43.8	48.9	48.3	35.9	42.1
Arkansas	43.8	47.5	39.5	45.5	42.7

TABLE 2-B *(continued)*

Average Rates of Voter Turnout in the States by Office, 1994–1997

State	Total	President	Governor	U.S. Senate	U.S. House
Illinois	43.6	49.2	35.7	48.5	41.0
Alabama	43.3	47.7	38.4	46.6	40.5
New Jersey	43.2	51.2	39.9	41.2	40.3
New Mexico	43.0	46.0	40.8	42.6	42.5
Pennsylvania	41.9	49.0	38.9	38.1	41.8
Tennessee	41.6	47.1	38.0	41.0	40.3
Virginia	41.5	47.5	33.8	43.8	40.8
Mississippi	41.3	45.6	41.8	38.4	39.4
Arizona	40.8	45.4	38.6	38.3	40.7
Hawaii	40.3	40.8	41.0	39.7	39.7
Kentucky	40.2	47.5	33.7	44.7	34.9
Maryland	40.1	46.7	37.6	36.5	39.5
Florida	39.7	48.0	38.7	37.8	34.4
West Virginia	39.7	45.0	44.5	36.2	33.1
New York	39.3	46.5	38.2	35.1	37.4
California	38.9	43.3	37.3	36.7	38.5
South Carolina	38.1	41.5	34.1	41.8	34.9
Georgia	37.3	42.6	30.0	41.9	34.6
Texas	36.4	41.2	33.2	36.5	34.8
Nevada	36.4	39.3	34.9	35.0	36.4
Average	46.0	50.8	43.9	45.7	43.8

SOURCE: Virginia Gray, Russell L. Hanson, and Herbert Jacob, *Politics in the American States: A Comparative Analysis, Seventh Edition* (Washington, D.C.: CQ Press, 1999), 100.

TABLE 2-C

Judicial Selection in the Fifty States

Partisan election	Nonpartisan election	Gubernatorial appointment	Legislative appointment	Merit Selection (Missouri Plan)
		All or most judgeships		
Alabama	Florida	California	South Carolina	Arizona
Arkansas	Georgia	Maine	Virginia	Alaska
Illinois	Idaho	New Hampshire	Colorado	
New York	Kentucky	New Jersey	Connecticut	
North Carolina	Louisiana		Delaware	
Pennsylvania	Michigan		Hawaii	
Tennessee	Minnesota		Indiana	
Texas	Mississippi		Iowa	
West Virginia	Montana		Kansas	
	Nevada		Maryland	
	North Dakota		Massachusetts	
	Ohio		Missouri	
	Oklahoma		Nebraska	
	Oregon		New Mexico	
	South Dakota		Rhode Island	
	Washington		Utah	
	Wisconsin		Vermont	
			Wyoming	
		Some judgeships		
Connecticut	Arizona	Montana	Rhode Island	Florida
Georgia	California	New York	New York	
Indiana	North Carolina	Oklahoma		
Maine		South Dakota		
Missouri		Tennessee		
South Carolina				

SOURCE: Virginia Gray, Russell L. Hanson, and Herbert Jacob, *Politics in the American States: A Comparative Analysis, Seventh Edition* (Washington, D.C.: CQ Press, 1999), 242.

TABLE 2-D

Types of Direct Primaries

Closed[a]	Semiclosed[b]	Semiopen[c]	Open[d]	Blanket[e]	Nonpartisan[f]
Arizona	*Voters may change*	*Voters must*	Hawaii	Alaska	Louisiana
Connecticut	*registration on*	*openly state in*	Idaho	California	
Delaware	*primary election day*	*which party*	Michigan	Washington	
Florida	Iowa	*primary they*	Minnesota		
Kentucky	Ohio	*wish to vote*	Montana		
Maryland	Wyoming	Alabama	North Dakota		
Nebraska	Arkansas	Utah			
Nevada	*Independents may*	Georgia	Vermont		
New Mexico	*register with a party*	Illinois	Wisconsin		
New York	*primary election day*	Indiana			
North Carolina	Massachusetts	Mississippi			
Oklahoma	New Hampshire	Missouri			
Oregon	South Carolina				
Pennsylvania	*Voters who have not*	Tennessee			
South Dakota	*previously voted in a*	Texas			
West Virginia	*party primary may*	Virginia			
	change registration				
	Colorado				
	Kansas				
	Maine				
	New Jersey				
	Rhode Island				

[a] Party registration required.

[b] Voters may register or change registration on election day.

[c] Public selection of a party required.

[d] Voter may vote in any party's primary.

[e] Voter may vote in more than one party's primary, but one candidate per office.

[f] Top two primary vote-getters, regardless of party, are nominated for general election.

SOURCE: Virginia Gray, Russell L. Hanson, and Herbert Jacob, *Politics in the American States: A Comparative Analysis, Seventh Edition* (Washington, D.C.: CQ Press, 1999), 88.

TABLE 2-E

Louisiana 2000 Presidential Exit Polls

	% of all	Gore	Bush
Are you:			
Male	45	39	56
Female	55	49	50
Are you:			
White	70	26	72
Black	29	92	6
Hispanic/Latino	1	0	0
Asian	0	0	0
Other	1	0	0
To which age group do you belong?			
18–29	19	38	57
30–44	32	44	54
45–59	27	44	53
60+	22	52	46
1999 total family income:			
Under $15,000	14	67	26
$15,000–$29,999	20	60	34
$30,000–$49,999	24	38	60
$50,000–$74,999	21	30	69
$75,000–$99,999	10	37	63
$100,000 or more	11	27	73

	% of all	Gore	Bush
No matter how you voted today, do you usually think of yourself as a:			
Democrat	48	74	24
Republican	34	6	92
Independent	18	31	61
Are you:			
Protestant/Christian	51	39	59
Catholic	38	41	57
Jewish	0	0	0
Other	7	70	23
None	3	0	0
Do you consider yourself part of the conservative Christian political movement known as the religious right?			
Yes	22	22	75
No	73	52	45
On most political matters, do you consider yourself:			
Liberal	18	73	22
Moderate	43	46	52
Conservative	39	24	74

SOURCE: ABC News.

TABLE 2-F

National 2000 Presidential Exit Polls

	% of all	Gore	Bush
Are you:			
Male	48	42	53
Female	52	54	43
Are you:			
White	81	42	54
Black	10	90	9
Hispanic/Latino	7	62	35
Asian	2	55	41
Other	1	55	39
To which age group do you belong?			
18–29	17	48	46
30–44	33	48	49
45–59	28	48	49
60+	22	51	47
1999 total family income:			
Under $15,000	7	57	37
$15,000–$29,999	16	54	41
$30,000–$49,999	24	49	48
$50,000–$74,999	25	46	51
$75,000–$99,999	13	45	52
$100,000 or more	15	43	54

	% of all	Gore	Bush
No matter how you voted today, do you usually think of yourself as a:			
Democrat	39	86	11
Republican	35	8	91
Independent	27	45	47
Are you:			
Protestant/Christian	54	42	56
Catholic	26	50	47
Jewish	4	79	19
Other	6	62	28
None	9	61	30
Do you consider yourself part of the conservative Christian political movement known as the religious right?			
Yes	14	18	80
No	83	54	42
On most political matters, do you consider yourself:			
Liberal	20	80	13
Moderate	50	52	44
Conservative	29	17	81

SOURCE: ABC News.

TABLE 3-A

Formal Powers of Governors

Very Strong	Strong	Moderate	Weak
New Jersey	Alaska	Indiana	Mississippi
Pennsylvania	Maine	Oregon	Texas
Utah	Montana	Rhode Island	South Carolina
Hawaii	Tennessee	Vermont	New Hampshire
Maryland	Arizona	Alabama	North Carolina
Massachusetts	Colorado	Arkansas	Nevada
Minnesota	Delaware	New Mexico	
New York	Idaho	Oklahoma	
	Iowa	Washington	
	California	Florida	
	Connecticut	Georgia	
	Illinois	Kansas	
	Michigan	Kentucky	
	South Dakota	**Louisiana**	
	Wyoming	North Dakota	
		West Virginia	
		Missouri	
		Nebraska	
		Ohio	
		Virginia	
		Wisconsin	

States listed in rank order of power within category.

SOURCE: Charles R. Adrien and Michael R. Fine, *State and Local Politics* (Chicago: Lyceum Books/Nelson Hall, 1991), 176. *Original Source:* Thad L. Beyle, "Governors" in *Politics in the American States: A Comparative Analysis,* ed. Virginia Gray, Herbert Jacob, and Kenneth N. Vines (Boston: Little, Brown, 1983), 202.

TABLE 3-B

Governors' Institutional Powers

State	SEP	TP	AP	BP	VP	PC	GIP
Alabama	1	4	2	3	4	2	2.7
Alaska	5	4	3.5	3	5	2	3.8
Arizona	1.5	4	2.5	3	5	4	3.3
Arkansas	2.5	4	2.5	3	4	1	2.8
California	1	4	3	3	5	2	3.0
Colorado	3	4	4	3	5	3	3.7
Connecticut	4	5	3	3	5	2	3.7
Delaware	2	4	3	3	5	3	3.3
Florida	3	4	1.5	3	5	2	3.1
Georgia	1	4	0.5	3	5	4	2.9
Hawaii	5	4	2.5	3	5	5	4.1
Idaho	2	5	2	3	5	5	3.7
Illinois	4	5	3	3	5	3	3.3
Indiana	3	4	4	3	2	3	3.2
Iowa	3	5	3	3	5	4	3.8
Kansas	3	4	3	3	5	4	3.7
Kentucky	3	4	3	3	4	4	3.5
Louisiana	1	4	3.5	3	5	2	3.1
Maine	5	4	3.5	3	4	1	3.4
Maryland	4	4	2.5	5	5	4	4.1
Massachusetts	4	4	1	3	5	1	3.0
Michigan	3	4	3.5	3	5	3	3.6
Minnesota	4	5	2.5	3	5	2	3.6
Mississippi	1	4	2	3	5	2	2.8
Missouri	2.5	4	2.5	3	5	4	3.5
Montana	3	4	2.5	3	5	4	3.6
Nebraska	3	4	3	4	5	3	3.7
Nevada	2.5	4	3.5	3	2	3	3.0
New Hampshire	5	2	3	3	2	2	2.8
New Jersey	5	4	3.5	3	5	4	4.1
New Mexico	3	4	4	3	5	2	3.5
New York	4	5	3.5	4	5	3	4.1
North Carolina	1	4	3	3	2	3	2.7
North Dakota	3	5	2.5	3	5	4	3.8
Ohio	4	4	4.5	3	5	4	4.1
Oklahoma	1	4	1	3	5	2	2.7
Oregon	2	4	2.5	3	5	2	3.1
Pennsylvania	4	4	4.5	3	5	2	4.1
Rhode Island	2.5	4	4	3	2	1	2.8
South Carolina	1	4	2	2	5	3	2.8
South Dakota	3	4	3.5	3	5	4	3.8
Tennessee	4.5	4	4	3	4	2	3.6
Texas	1	5	3.5	2	5	3	3.3
Utah	4	4.5	3.5	3	5	4	4.0
Vermont	2.5	2	4	3	2	4	2.9
Virginia	2.5	3	3.5	3	5	3	3.3
Washington	1	4	2.5	3	5	2	2.9
West Virginia	2.5	4	4.5	5	5	2	3.8
Wisconsin	3	5	2	3	5	4	3.7
Wyoming	2	4	3.5	3	5	4	3.6
50 state avg.	2.8	4.1	3.0	3.1	4.5	3.0	3.4

SEP: Separately elected executive branch officials: 5 = only governor or governor/lieutenant governor team elected; 4.5 = governor or governor/lieutenant governor team, with one other elected official; 4 = governor/lieutenant governor team with some process officials (attorney general, secretary of state, treasurer, auditor) elected; 3 = governor/lieutenant governor team with process officials, and some major and minor policy officials elected; 2.5 = governor (no team) with six or fewer officials elected, but none are major policy officials; 2 = governor (no team) with six or fewer officials elected, including one major policy official; 1.5 = governor (no team) with six or fewer officials elected, but two are major policy officials; 1 = governor (no team) with seven or more process and several major policy officials elected. [*Original source:* CSG, (1996, 33–9)]

TP: Tenure potential of governors: 5 = four-year term, no restraint on reelection; 4.5 = four-year term, only three terms permitted; 4 = four-year term, only two terms permitted; 3 = four-year term, no consecutive reelection permitted; 2 = two-year term, no restraint on reelection. [*Original source:* CSG (1996, 17–8)]

AP: Governor's appointment powers in six major functional areas: corrections, K–12 education, health, highways/transportation, public utilities regulation, and welfare. The six individual office scores are totaled and then averaged and rounded to the nearest .5 for the state score. That average score is then rounded to the nearest .5 between 0 and 5. 5 = governor appoints, no other approval needed; 4 = governor appoints, a board, council, or legislature approves; 3 = someone else appoints, governor approves or shares appointment; 2 = someone else appoints, governor and others approve; 1 = someone else appoints, no approval or confirmation needed. [*Original source:* CSG (1996, 35–9)]

BP: Governor's budgetary power: 5 = governor has full responsibility; legislature may not increase executive budget; 4 = governor has full responsibility; legislature can increase special majority vote or subject to item veto; 3 = governor has full responsibility; legislature has unlimited power to change executive budget; 2 = governor shares responsibility; legislature has unlimited power to change executive budget. [*Original Source:* CSG (1996, 228–9; NCSL (1998a)]

VP: Governor's veto power: 5 = has the item veto and a special majority vote of the legislature is needed to override a veto (three-fifths of legislators elected or two-thirds of legislators present); 4 = has item veto with a majority of the legislators elected needed to override; 3 = has item veto with only a majority of the legislators present needed to override; 2 = no item veto power. [*Original source:* CSG (1996, 22–3, 98–9)]

PC: Gubernatorial party control: the governor's party: 5 = has a substantial majority (75 percent or more) in both houses of the legislature; 4 = has a simple majority in both houses (less than 75 percent), or a substantial majority in one house and a simple majority in the other; 3 = split party control in the legislature or a nonpartisan legislature; 2 = simple majority in both houses, or a simple minority (25 percent or more) in one and a substantial minority (less than 25 percent) in the other; 1 = substantial minority in both houses. [*Original source:* NCSL (1998b)]

GIP: Governor's institutional powers score: The sum of the scores for SEP, TP, AP, BP, VP, and PC divided by 6 to stay within the 5-point format. Overall power score rounded to nearest tenth of a point.

SOURCE: Virginia Gray, Russell L. Hanson, and Herbert Jacob, *Politics in the American States: A Comparative Analysis, Seventh Edition* (Washington, D.C.: CQ Press, 1999), 210–11.

TABLE 3-C

Classification of the Fifty States According to the Overall Impact of Interest Groups in the Late 1990s

Dominant (5)	Dominant/ Complementary (25)	Complementary (16)	Complementary/ Subordinate (4)	Subordinate (0)
Alabama	Arizona	Colorado	Minnesota	
Florida	Arkansas	Delaware	Rhode Island	
Nevada	Alaska	Indiana	South Dakota	
South Carolina	California	Hawaii	Vermont	
West Virginia	Connecticut	Maine		
	Georgia	Massachusetts		
	Idaho	Michigan		
	Illinois	Missouri		
	Iowa	New Hampshire		
	Kansas	New Jersey		
	Kentucky	New York		
	Louisiana	North Carolina		
	Maryland	North Dakota		
	Mississippi	Pennsylvania		
	Montana	Utah		
	Nebraska	Wisconsin		
	New Mexico			
	Ohio			
	Oklahoma			
	Oregon			
	Tennessee			
	Texas			
	Virginia			
	Washington			
	Wyoming			

SOURCE: Virginia Gray, Russell L. Hanson, and Herbert Jacob, *Politics in the American States: A Comparative Analysis, Seventh Edition* (Washington, D.C.: CQ Press, 1999), 137. Compiled by the authors from the 1998 update of the Hrebenar-Thomas study.

TABLE 3-D

Louisiana Interest Group Ratings

Strongest	Next strongest
La. Association of Business and Industry	La. Association of Educators
La. Association of Trial Lawyers	La. Federation of Teachers
La. Chemical Association	La. Municipal Association
oil and gas industry	La. Police Jury Association*
wholesalers and retailers	gambling industry
La. AFL-CIO	seafood industry
La. Farm Bureau	Council for a Better La.**
	liquor & beverage companies

*County government officials in rural parishes

**Public interest group

SOURCE: Compiled by the author for the 1998 update of the Hrebenar-Thomas study.

TABLE 4-A
Ed Renwick's Twenty People Who Influenced Louisiana

JOHN ALARIO, former state Speaker of the House

JOHN BREAUX, U.S. senator

VICTOR BUSSIE, former AFL-CIO president

LAWRENCE A. CHEHARDY, former Jefferson Parish assessor

KIRBY DUCOTE, executive director of the Louisiana Catholic Conference

DAVID DUKE, former state representative

EDWIN EDWARDS, governor

CLEO FIELDS, state senator and former U.S. congressman

MURPHY J. "MIKE" FOSTER, governor

RANDY HAYNIE, lobbyist

E. L. "BUBBA" HENRY, lobbyist and former state Speaker of the House

PAUL HURD, attorney who sued to have the black Second Congressional District redrawn

LESLIE JACOBS, Foster appointee to the state Board of Elementary and Secondary Education

J. BENNETT JOHNSTON, former U.S. senator

EDDIE JORDAN JR., U.S. attorney for Louisiana who prosecuted Edwin Edwards

DAN JUNEAU, present director of the Louisiana Association of Business and Industry (LABI)

JAMES "JIM BOB" MOFFETT, Louisiana businessman and lobbyist

ERNEST N. "DUTCH" MORIAL, former mayor of New Orleans

BOB ODOM, Louisiana commissioner of agriculture

BUDDY ROEMER, governor

ED STEIMEL, former director of LABI

PATRICK TAYLOR, Louisiana businessman and education activist

DAVE TREEN, governor

JOHN VOLZ, former U.S. attorney who prosecuted Edwin Edwards

SOURCE: *Louisiana Life* (autumn 2001): 50–5.

TABLE 5-A

Louisiana Ranking on the Lists

Louisiana is among HIGHEST *(top ten) on these lists:*

Population in Poverty, 1999	2nd
Death Rates (age-adjusted), 1998	2nd
Unemployed and Unemployment Rate, 2000	9th
Gambling, 1997	5th
Annual Electricity Use per Residential Customer, 1999	2nd
Hunters with Firearms, 1999	8th
Toxic Chemical Release, 1998	3rd
Polluted Rivers and Streams, 1998	4th
Sales Taxes, FY 1997	5th
Sales Tax Revenue as a Percentage of Three-Tax Revenue, FY 1997	4th
Students in Private Schools, 1997–1998	3rd
Infant Mortality Rates, 1996–1998	3rd
Percentage of Non-elderly Population without Health Insurance, 1999	3rd
Alcohol Consumption per Capita, 1997	9th
Percentage of Population Overweight, 1999	4th
AIDS Cases, 1999	9th
Total Crime Rate, 1999	4th
Violent Crime Rate, 1999	6th
Murder and Rape Rates, 1999	**1st**
Property Crime Rates, 1999	4th
Incarceration Rate, 1999	**1st**
Traffic Deaths per 100 Million Vehicle Miles, 1999	4th
Average Hourly Earnings, 2000	8th

Louisiana is among LOWEST *(bottom ten) on these lists:*

Labor Force, 2000	49th
Fortune 500 Companies, 2000	40th
Exports, 1999	5th
Workers' Compensation Temporary Disability Payments, 2000	46th
Index of State Economic Momentum, September 2000	49th
Percentage of Households with Computers, 2000	48th

State Park Acreage, FY 1999	45th
State Park Visitors, FY 1999	50th
Units of Government, 1997	46th
Social Security Benefits Paid, 1998	49th
Federal Tax Burden, Total and per Capita, FY 2000	42nd
Property Taxes, FY 1997	48th
Property Taxes per Capita, FY 1997	47th
Tax Burden on Wealthy Families, 1998	49th
Percentage of Population over 25 with a High School Diploma, 1999	46th
High School Completion Rates, 1997–1999	44th
Avg. Salary of Assoc. Professors at "Flagship" State Universities, 1999–2000	44th
State Health Rankings, 2000	49th
Condition of Children Index, 2000	**50th**

Compiled by author from Kendra Hovey and Harold Hovey, *CQ's State Fact Finder 2001: Rankings across America* (Washington, D.C.: CQ Press, 2001), pages in order reported (highest) 28, 32, 49, 69, 70, 85, 79, 91, 150, 152, 202, 229, 231, 233, 235, 236, 252, 253, 254, 255, 260, 275, 43; (lowest) 48, 53, 56, 63, 65, 73, 82, 83, 101, 128, 132, 147, 148, 161, 201, 203, 219, 230, 291.

TABLE 5-B

Major Sources of State Revenue

	Millions of dollars	Percent
Sales and Use Taxes	2,405.0	37
Individual Income Tax	1,654.0	25
Gaming Revenue	583.3	9
Corporate Taxes	571.0	9
Gasoline and Special Fuels	553.0	8
Mineral Revenue	511.1	8
Miscellaneous Taxes and Fees	268.0	4

Estimated for the Fiscal Year 1999–2000 by the Revenue Estimating Conference on May 6, 1999.

SOURCE: Louisiana House of Representatives House Legislative Services, *State and Local Government in Louisiana: An Overview, 2000–2004 Term*, 79.

Notes

1. Political Culture

1. V. O. Key Jr., *Southern Politics in State and Nation* (New York, 1949).
2. Alexander Lamis, ed., *Southern Politics in the 1990s* (Baton Rouge, 1999).
3. Key, *Southern Politics,* 156.
4. Jack Bass and Walter DeVries, *The Transformation of Southern Politics: Social Change and Political Consequences since 1945* (New York, 1976), 159.
5. Tyler Bridges, *Bad Bet on the Bayou: The Rise of Gambling in Louisiana and the Fall of Governor Edwin Edwards* (New York, 2001), 4.
6. Alexis de Tocqueville, *Democracy in America,* trans., ed., and with an introduction by Harvey C. Mansfield and Delba Winthrop (Chicago, 2000).
7. Ibid.
8. Daniel J. Elazar, *American Federalism: A View from the States* (New York, 1966).
9. Cecil Eubanks, "The South: Change and Continuity," in *The Political Transformation of the South,* ed. James Lea (Baton Rouge, 1988), 292.
10. Ibid. (emphasis added).
11. Ibid., 291.
12. C. Vann Woodward, *The Burden of Southern History* (Baton Rouge, 1960), 190.
13. W. J. Cash, *The Mind of the South* (New York, 1941); Twelve Southerners, *I'll Take My Stand: The South and the Agrarian Tradition* (1930; reprint Baton Rouge, 1977).
14. Cash, *Mind of the South,* 440.
15. George Tindall, "Mythic South," in *Encyclopedia of Southern Culture,* ed. Charles Reagan Wilson and William Ferris, 4 vols. (New York, 1991), 3:443.
16. http://roadsidegeorgia.com/links/history/civilwar/people/sherman http://roadsidegeorgia.com/int/515.
17. Mitford M. Mathews, ed., *A Dictionary of Americanisms on Historical Principles* (Chicago, 1951).
18. D. L. A. Hackett, "The Social Structure of Jacksonian Louisiana," in *Readings in Louisiana Politics,* ed. Mark T. Carleton, Perry H. Howard, and Joseph B. Parker (2nd ed.; Baton Rouge, 1988), 144.
19. Lisa Baker, *The Second Battle of New Orleans* (New York, 1996), 13.
20. Lewis William Newton, "Creoles and Anglo-Americans in Old Louisiana—A Study in Cultural Conflict," in *Readings in Louisiana Politics,* ed. Carleton, Howard, and Parker, 72.
21. Baker, *Second Battle of New Orleans,* 4.
22. Ibid., 13–4.
23. Charles Grenier, "The Political Mobilization of the Black Electorate in Louisiana, 1932–1980," in *Readings in Louisiana Politics,* ed. Carleton, Howard, and Parker, 513–4.

24. Jewell L. Prestage and Carolyn Sue Williams, "Blacks in Louisiana Politics," in *Louisiana Politics: Festival in a Labyrinth,* ed. James Bolner (Baton Rouge, 1982), 289.
25. Wayne Parent and Wesley Shrum, "Critical Electoral Success and Black Voter Registration: An Elaboration of the Voter Consent Model," *Social Science Quarterly* 66 (1985): 695–703.
26. Grenier, "Political Mobilization of the Black Electorate," 531.
27. As quoted in Hackett, "Social Structure of Jacksonian Democracy," 145.
28. Charles Dew, "Who Won the Secession Election in Louisiana?" *Journal of Southern History* 36 (1970): 18.
29. Ibid.
30. Ibid.
31. David Landry and Joseph Parker, "The Louisiana Political Culture," in *Louisiana Politics,* ed. Bolner, 2.
32. Ibid., 3.
33. Ibid., 2.
34. Stephan Caldas, "The Politics of Welfare Reform, Religion, Education, and Racism: Evidence from Three Southern Elections," *Southern Studies* 3 (1992): 1–14.
35. Earl Black and Merle Black, *Politics and Society in the South* (Cambridge, Mass., 1987).
36. "How We Voted and Why, " *New Orleans Times-Picayune,* November 19, 1995, A-20.
37. William Ivy Hair, "Rob Them! You Bet!" in *Readings in Louisiana Politics,* ed. Carleton, Howard, and Parker, 333, 337.
38. C. Vann Woodward, *Origins of the New South* (Baton Rouge, 1951), 343.
39. Merl Reed, "Louisiana's Economy in the 1830s," in *Readings in Louisiana Politics,* ed. Carleton, Howard, and Parker, 122–37.
40. Raymond Strother in a film by the Center for New American Media, in association with Louisiana Public Broadcasting, *Louisiana Boys: Raised on Politics* (1991).
41. T. Harry Williams, "The Gentleman from Louisiana: Demagogue or Democrat," *Journal of Southern History* 26 (February 1960): 7.
42. Ibid., 6–8.
43. As quoted by Jo Ann Carrigan in "Realism and Corruption in Louisiana Politics," in *Readings in Louisiana Politics,* ed. Carleton, Howard, and Parker, 62.
44. Robert Mann, *Legacy to Power: Senator Russell Long of Louisiana* (New York, 1992), 53–4.
45. Bridges, *Bad Bet on the Bayou,* 6.
46. Edwin Edwards in Center for New American Media, *Louisiana Boys.*
47. Key, *Southern Politics,* 156.
48. Center for New American Media, *Louisiana Boys.*
49. Michael Barone and Grant Ujifusa, *Almanac of American Politics 1994* (New York, 1994), 528.
50. Gus Weill in Center for New American Media, *Louisiana Boys.*

2. Participation

1. Michael L. Kurtz and Morgan D. Peoples, *Earl K. Long: The Saga of Uncle Earl and Louisiana Politics* (Baton Rouge, 1990), 186.
2. Ibid., 187.
3. In fact the politics did change in 2002. Louisiana will no longer elect a commissioner of elec-

tions. See chap. 5 for a full discussion of the change.

4. Thomas Dye, *Politics in States and Communities* (Upper Saddle River, N.J., 2000), 232.

5. Ed Anderson, "Judicial Elections to Be Ordered This Fall," *New Orleans Times-Picayune*, July 8, 1991, B-1.

6. "State Invites Suit," ibid., September 21, 1991, B-1.

7. John Maginnis, *The Last Hayride* (Baton Rouge, 1984), 334.

8. Ibid.

9. Raymond Strother in Center for New American Media, *Louisiana Boys.*

10. John Maginnis, *Cross to Bear* (Baton Rouge, 1992), 104.

11. Ibid., 104–105.

12. Edward Renwick, T. Wayne Parent, and Jack Wardlaw, "Louisiana: Still Sui Generis Like Huey," in *Southern Politics in the 1990s*, ed. Alexander Lamis (Baton Rouge, 1999), 283.

13. Dew, "Who Won the Secession Election in Louisiana?" 18.

14. Darron Shaw, "The Methods behind the Madness: Presidential Electoral College Preferences, 1984–1996," *Journal of Politics* 61 (November 1999): 903.

15. Norman Sherman, Louisiana State University Manship School of Mass Communication "Media and Politics" lecture series, March 22, 2000, Old State Capitol, Baton Rouge.

16. Edward Pratt, "Hannan Creates a Political Stir," *Baton Rouge Advocate*, November 2, 1996, 7-B.

17. Author interview with Jeff Palermo, March 11, 2003.

3. Government

1. T. Harry Williams, *Huey Long* (New York, 1970); Robert Penn Warren, *All the King's Men* (New York, 1990).

2. Williams, *Huey Long*, 3.

3. Ibid.

4. Alan Brinkley, *Voices of Protest: Huey Long, Father Coughlin, and the Great Depression* (New York, 1983), 21.

5. Ibid., 22.

6. A. J. Liebling, *The Earl of Louisiana* (1961; reprint Baton Rouge, 1970), 91.

7. Ibid., 21.

8. Kurtz and Peoples, *Earl K. Long*, 211–2.

9. Ibid., 255.

10. Liebling, *Earl of Louisiana*, 4.

11. Ibid.

12. Marshall McLuhan, *Understanding Media: The Extensions of Man* (1964; reprint Boston, 1994).

13. Maginnis, *Last Hayride.*

14. Maginnis, *Cross to Bear*, 43.

15. Ibid., 11.

16. Ibid., 13.

17. Hrebenar and Thomas, eds., *Interest Group Politics in the Southern States*, 306.

18. Melinda Gann Hall, "Constituent Influence in State Supreme Courts: Conceptual Notes in a Case Study," *Journal of Politics* 49 (1987): 1123.

4. Local Politics

1. Mann, *Legacy to Power,* 81.
2. "Plaquemines Parish Page Locale Online," http://www.lapage.com/parishes/plaqu.htm.
3. Robert Sherrill, *Gothic Politics in the Deep South* (New York, 1968), 8.
4. Glen Jeansonne, *Leander Perez: Boss of the Delta* (Baton Rouge, 1977), 24.
5. Ibid., 76.
6. James Conaway, *Judge: The Life and Times of Leander Perez* (New York, 1973), 24–5.
7. Jeansonne, *Leander Perez,* 225.
8. Leander Perez, "The Challenge to the South and How It Must Be Met," speech given at Biloxi, Miss., July 21, unspecified year.
9. Conaway, *Judge,* 161.
10. Jeansonne, *Leander Perez,* 363.
11. Ed Renwick, "Power Players: Twenty People Who Influenced Louisiana, 1981–2001," *Louisiana Life,* autumn 2001, 50–5.
12. Renwick, *Louisiana Life,* 51.
13. Richard Engstrom, "Home Rule in Louisiana—Could This Be the Promised Land?" *Louisiana History* (1975), 431–55.
14. Calvin Trillin, "New Orleans Unmasked," *New Yorker,* February 2, 1998, 38.
15. James Gill, *Lords of Misrule: Mardi Gras and the Politics of Race in New Orleans* (Jackson, Miss., 1997).
16. (http://216.239.51.104/search?q=cache:EHdlSmuueqsJ:www.mardigrasdigest.com/Sec_mgind/history.htm+Mardi+Gras+Indians&hl=en&ie=UTF-8).
17. Official Zulu website, http://www.mardigrasneworleans.com/zulu/main.html
18. Baker, *Second Battle of New Orleans,* 4.
19. Robert L. Crain, *The Politics of School Desegregation* (Chicago, 1968), 237.
20. Ibid., 263–4.
21. Baker, *Second Battle of New Orleans,* 379.
22. Crain, *Politics of School Desegregation,* 280.
23. Ibid., 269–74.
24. Ibid., 276.
25. Ibid., 282.
26. Ibid., 283–4.
27. Trillin, "New Orleans Unmasked," 43.
28. Nicolas Lemann, "Hard Times in the Big Easy," *Harper's,* August 1987, 18.
29. Ed Haas, "Political Continuity in the Crescent City: Toward an Interpretation of New Orleans Politics, 1874–1986," *Louisiana History* 39:1 (1998):16.
30. Editorial, "Houston Is Growing Too," *Baton Rouge Morning Advocate,* August 5, 1947, 4.
31. Hank Braden in Center for New American Media, *Louisiana Boys.*
32. "The Handbook of Texas Online: Commission Form of City Government," http://www.tsha.utexas.edu/handbook/online/articles/view/CC/moc1.html.
33. Author interview with John Hussey, May 13, 2002.
34. Ibid.

35. Author interview with Lanny Keller, May 14, 2002.

36. Crain, *Politics of School Desegregation,* 139.

5. Change

1. "Foster Explains Grandfather's Role in 1896 Segregation Law," *Baton Rouge Advocate,* March 5, 2002, 12-A.

2. Adam Faircloth, *Race and Democracy: The Civil Rights Struggle in Louisiana, 1915–1972* (Athens, Ga., 1995), xx.

3. Ralph David Abernathy, *And the Walls Came Tumbling Down* (New York, 1989), 178.

4. Martin Luther King, "Stride toward Freedom: The Montgomery Story," in *A Martin Luther King Treasury* (Yonkers, N.Y., 1964), 55–6.

5. Peter Jan Honigsberg, *Crossing Border Street: A Civil Rights Memoir* (Berkeley, 2000).

6. Wayne Parent and Huey Perry, "Louisiana: African Americans, Republicans, and Party Competition," in *The New Politics of the Old South,* ed. Charles S. Bullock III and Mark J. Rozell (Lanham, Md., 1998), 118.

7. Trillin, "New Orleans Unmasked," 46.

8. CODOFIL website: http://www.codofil.org/english/index.html.

9. "Census Concludes French Heritage Fading in Louisiana," *Baton Rouge Advocate,* May 25, 2002, 4-B.

10. Ibid.

11. Ibid.

12. William B. McMahon, "David Duke and the Legislature," in *The Emergence of David Duke and the Politics of Race,* ed. Douglas Rose (Chapel Hill, 1992), 124.

13. "How We Voted and Why," *New Orleans Times-Picayune,* November 19, 1995, A-1.

14. Charles Barrilleaux and Charles Hadley, "'The Final Throes of Freewheeling Ways?" in *Interest Group Politics in the Southern States,* ed. Ronald J. Hrebenar and Clive Thomas (Tuscaloosa, 1992), 305.

15. Chris Gautreau, "Ed Steimel Rips into Business Interests," *Baton Rouge Advocate,* October 31, 2001.

16. Chris Frink, "Governor Lashes Business Lobby for Pushing Tax Cuts," *Baton Rouge Advocate,* April 30, 2002, 1-A.

17. "Old Alabama Won't Leave Politely," *Economist,* May 22, 2002, http://www.economist.com/diversions/displaystory.cfm?story_id=1035137.

18. Alan Ehrenhart, "Assessments: Electoral Overload," in *Governing,* August 2001, www.governing.com/archive/2001/aug/assess.txt.

Selected Readings

SOUTHERN POLITICS AND CULTURE *(General)*

Applebome, Peter. *Dixie Rising.* San Diego: Harcourt Brace, 1997.

Black, Earl, and Merle Black. *Politics and Society in the South.* Cambridge: Harvard University Press, 1987.

Cash, W. J. *The Mind of the South.* New York: A. A. Knopf, 1941.

Eagles, Charles. *Is There a Southern Political Tradition?* Jackson: University Press of Mississippi, 1996.

Lea, James, ed. *The Political Transformation of the South.* Baton Rouge: Louisiana State University Press, 1988.

Twelve Southerners. *I'll Take My Stand: The South and the Agrarian Tradition.* Baton Rouge: Louisiana State University Press, 1977.

SOUTHERN POLITICS WITH LOUISIANA-SPECIFIC CHAPTERS

Bass, Jack, and Walter DeVries. *The Transformation of Southern Politics: Social Change and Political Consequences since 1945.* New York: Basic Books, 1976.

Black, Earl, and Merle Black. *The Rise of Southern Republicans.* Cambridge: Belknap Press, 2002.

Bullock, Charles S. III, and Mark J. Rozell, eds. *The New Politics of the Old South.* Lanham, Md.: Rowman & Littlefield, 2003.

Hrebenar, Ronald J., and Clive Thomas, eds. *Interest Group Politics in the Southern States.* Tuscaloosa: University of Alabama Press, 1992

Key, V. O. *Southern Politics in State and Nation.* New York: Vintage Books, 1949.

Lamis, Alexander, ed. *Southern Politics in the 1990s.* Baton Rouge: Louisiana State University Press, 1999.

COMPARATIVE STATE POLITICS

Beyle, Thad. *State and Local Government 2001–2002.* Washington, D.C.: CQ Press, 2001.

Bowman, Ann, and Richard Kearney. *State and Local Government.* Boston: Houghton Mifflin, 2002.
Dye, Thomas. *Politics in States and Communities.* Upper Saddle River, N.J.: Prentice Hall, 2000.
Elazar, Daniel J. *American Federalism: A View from the States.* New York: Crowell, 1966.
Gray, Virginia, Russell L. Hanson, and Herbert Jacob. *Politics in the American States: A Comparative Analysis.* Washington, D.C.: CQ Press, 1999.
Van Horn, Carl. *The State of the States.* Washington, D.C.: CQ Press, 1996.

RACE POLITICS IN LOUISIANA

Baker, Lisa. *The Second Battle of New Orleans.* New York: HarperCollins, 1996.
Crain, Robert L. *The Politics of School Desegregation.* Chicago: Aldine, 1968.
Faircloth, Adam. *Race and Democracy: The Civil Rights Struggle in Louisiana, 1915–1972.* Athens: University of Georgia Press, 1995.
Gill, James. *Lords of Misrule: Mardi Gras and the Politics of Race in New Orleans.* Jackson: University Press of Mississippi, 1997.
Honigsberg, Peter Jan. *Crossing Border Street: A Civil Rights Memoir.* Berkeley: University of California Press, 2000.

LOUISIANA POLITICIANS

Bridges, Tyler. *Bad Bet on the Bayou: The Rise of Gambling in Louisiana and the Fall of Governor Edwin Edwards.* New York: Farrar, Straus, and Giroux, 2001.
Brinkley, Alan. *Voices of Protest: Huey Long, Father Coughlin, and the Great Depression.* New York: Knopf, 1982.
Conaway, James. *Judge: The Life and Times of Leander Perez.* New York: Knopf, 1973.
Jeansonne, Glen. *Leander Perez: Boss of the Delta.* Baton Rouge: Louisiana State University Press, 1977.
Kane, Harnett T., and Sam H. Jones. *Louisiana Hayride.* Gretna, La.: Pelican, 1990.
Kurtz, Michael, and Morgan Peoples. *Earl K. Long: The Saga of Uncle Earl and Louisiana Politics.* Baton Rouge: Louisiana State University Press, 1990.

Liebling, A. J. *The Earl of Louisiana.* Baton Rouge: Louisiana State University Press, 1970.

Mann, Robert. *Legacy to Power: Senator Russell Long of Louisiana.* New York: Paragon House, 1992.

Rose, Douglas, ed. *The Emergence of David Duke and the Politics of Race.* Chapel Hill: University of North Carolina Press, 1992.

Sindler, Allan P. *Huey Long's Louisiana: State Politics, 1920–1952.* Baltimore: Johns Hopkins University Press, 1968.

Williams, T. Harry. *Huey Long.* New York: Bantam Books, 1970.

LOUISIANA ELECTIONS

Maginnis, John. *Cross to Bear.* Baton Rouge: Darkhorse Press, 1992

———. *The Last Hayride.* Baton Rouge: Gris Gris Press, 1984.

Index